EARNED ACREAGE

EARNED ACREAGE

TED L. GRAGG

CONNIE B. GRAGG

This book is a work of fiction. Many of the place names, cities, and well-known historical figures are real and integral to the story as it occurs within known histories of the United States of America. Names of businesses, some characters, as well as some of the places and incidents are the products of the author's imagination.

Copyright © 2025 by Ted L Gragg

All rights reserved, including the right of reproduction in whole or in part in any form. All rights reserved worldwide. No portion of this book may be published or transmitted in any form or any means, electronic or mechanical including photocopy, recording, or any information or storage retrieval system without written permission from the publisher.

The Library of Congress has cataloged the original edition as follows:

Ted L. Gragg with Connie B. Gragg

Earned Acreage

ISBN 978-0-9794572-8-9

0-9794572-8-9

Printed in the United States of America

First Printing 2025

Flat River Rock Publishing Division

First Printing, 2025

Dedicated to the spirit of America and its pioneers

CONTENTS

Photo Insert   ii
Copyright   iv
Dedication   v

One	Alex Bowie Avery	1
Two	Billy Rudd	12
Three	Lieutenant Preston Winston Francine	16
Four	Tobias Walking Horse	30
Five	Poinsettia Posey Vaughn	36
Six	Monique Mona Vaughn	49
Seven	Herman The German	53
Eight	Storm Cloud	70
Nine	Jessie McGregor	74
Ten	The Bear	81
Eleven	Water Barrel	86
Twelve	Table Talk	94
Thirteen	Hostiles	102
Fourteen	Westward Ho!	109
Fifteen	Percival O'Grady	115
Sixteen	Banks Of The Red River	125

Seventeen	Rescue	130
Eighteen	Nacogdoches	149
Nineteen	Samuel Sambo	160
Twenty	Wounded Foot	180
Twenty One	Ignacio	206
Twenty Two	Cortez	210
Twenty Three	Lancers	218
	Photo Insert	232

CHAPTER ONE

Alex Bowie Avery

The youngest Avery son kicked a dirt clod out of the cornfield row. Angrily he stomped another clump of dirt that lay in front of his feet, smashing it to bits of dust.

"Dirt, dirt, dirt, and more dirt," he thought. "Hoe the dirt, plow the dirt, shovel the dirt, plant seeds in the dirt! There's no end to working the dirt on this farm." Alex Bowie Avery brushed the dirt from his hands, wiped a dusty sleeve across his perspiring forehead, and headed for the big house and his mama Taggan's kitchen. Except it wasn't mama Taggan's anymore. Taggan, his mother, had died three years ago and now the house and its kitchen was his sister Caroline's, hers and their brother Nimrod Avery.

He scrapped the soles of his boots on the bristly mud mat outside the door and stomped into the kitchen's antechamber. Alex lifted the dipper out of the water bucket on the bench by the door and slurped the cool water down his parched throat. He flung drops of water from the dipper through the outside doorway, thrust the dipper back into the water pail, and stomped on into the kitchen.

His sister Carolina had her back turned to him as he entered the kitchen. Alex stood straight, flung his shoulders back, and spoke loudly in her direction.

"I've had enough of the farm's dirt. It's yours and Nimrod's anyway as the eldest children. Me, I'm going to war. Gonna take my horse and ride to Traveler's Rest in the upstate and enlist. Word's floating about that Colonel Reuben Nash is recruiting men to form the South Carolina Volunteers. I'm old enough now, I'm 18, and I've decided to leave in the morning. No more hoeing, no more planting, no more dirt. I'm outta here!"

His sister just turned and looked at him. Finally, hands on her hips, she glared at Alex and said,

"Alright, little Brother, if that's what you want. You know our Da's not been right in his head since mama died. You know that he can't take care of this farm, can't even take care of himself. I have to guide him just to let him gather the eggs. But if you want to leave, just go ahead. Nimrod and I will handle your share of the work and caring for Da. But, if you go, you'll need some money to take with you. So, after the dinner meal, Nimrod and I will just buy your share of the farm, give you some coin, and you just go on and do your warring."

Alex was awake before dawn. He saddled his mare and put a bridle with a lead rope on one of the farm's Marsh Tackys, then lashed his pack and gear to the sturdy horse's back.

Nimrod and Carolina came out of the farmhouse just as Alex completed packing and saddling the horses.

"Some biscuits and ham, Alex. There's enough wrapped in the napkins to get you through to our kinfolks, the Rudds, up in Pendleton. Put these in your saddlebags." Caroline said as she handed the food to him.

Alex mounted his bay mare. Nimrod handed him up a musket, along with a leather possibles bag filled with musket balls, spare flints, patches, and a fire steel striker along with an old tomahawk.

"The tomahawk was our Da's. He carried it during the Revolutionary War. Since you're insistent on joining up for this 1812 stirring, we thought that you might have use for it, little brother."

Alex looked at his older siblings. "I love you both," he said, "And we'll always be family, kin."

"God be with you, Alex. Be safe and remember to seek the Lord in times of trouble or doubt." Carolina touched Alex's knee, turned, and ran toward the house. She stopped suddenly and turned around and said as an after thought, "Don't forget to write occasionally; keep us informed as to your well-being."

"Best go on, brother. She's taking your leaving hard. We'll take care of Da. Be gone now and do travel safe." Nimrod slapped the mare's flank, starting Alex on his quest.

Alex rode into the village of Pendleton on the afternoon of the sixth day. He inquired of a villager leaning on a split-rail fence the location of the Rudd farm.

"Ye must be a stranger bout these parts for sure." The leaner squinted up at the young rider leading a small pack horse. "Look yonder." The lazy leaner pointed toward the west. "See that tall granary with the red roof off there in the distance. Looks sort of small from here, but be assured it's full growed when you fetch up to it. That's Will Rudd's place." The leaner pushed up from his leaning position, turned, and walked away.

Alex rode toward the red roofed silo. He rode through the farm's gate and halted in the barnyard. The ground-broke mare stood where Alex had dismounted and rolled her eyes in his direction as he approached the farmhouse.

A serving girl opened the front door and led him to a large sitting room. A cheerful fire crackled in the room's fireplace. A man in his stocking feet came across the room.

Hand out, he spoke first. "I'm William Rudd. Just whom do I have the pleasure of addressing?"

"Alex Bowie Avery, Uncle William. I'm Bowie Avery's younger son, from the Hickory Grove down on the coast near Kingston. I'm on the way to Traveler's Rest to join the army that's forming. I bring my kin's regards to you and your family." Alex doffed his hat and bowed.

"Welcome, lad, welcome. How're the folks back down on the coast. Well, I hope. Tell you what, you can tell me about them all while we unsaddle and stable your animals." William led the way, stopping in the hallway to pull on his boots. "C'mon. We've just enough time to grain and brush down your horses before supper time."

Uncle William hung Alex'x saddle on the rest next to one of the stalls. "Now, how are the folks?"

Alex rubbed his chin. "Sir, you recall that Ma, Taggan, passed away almost three years ago. Well, Dad, Bowie, your brother-in-law, he hasn't always been in his right mind since Mama died. But my older sister Caroline and my brother Nimrod take good care of him. I sold them my share of the old homeplace. I don't do well behind a plow. So, I decided to join up. That's why I'm here."

William looked his nephew square in the eye. "I think I understand that. If my memory is correct, your Pa didn't waste much time before he joined the Revolutionary effort back in 75'. Must run in the family. Well, no matter. You are here now and its almost meal time. Let's wash the grime off and go join the others for the evening meal."

That evening around the supper table, Billy Rudd II popped the question to his father William and his mother Patricia.

"You know, Papa, I turn 18 in a couple of weeks. I've been listening to Alex and I'd like to enlist along with him. What say you, Father, and Ma. Could I go along with my cousin?"

Agreement was soon delivered to the young men. Billy left the table, excited, and began to prepare his things for the day's ride to Traveler's Rest on the morrow.

The two young men, cousins, had both taken the oath of allegiance to the United States on the eve of the following day. And, since neither of them had ever served, neither were granted officer status but instead were assigned as infantrymen. As such their horses and the Marsh Tacky pack horse were confiscated. And, there was still a lot of dirt...and mud...and rain...and more dirt. The two young men and others like them slept on the cold ground, shoveled in the dirt building fortifications, and some cases serving as members of a burial party after an engagement for months.

"Here it is now in early April, 1814." Alex pondered. "And I'm still in the dirt." Alex Bowie Avery lay on his belly, arms outstretched in front, his left hand grasping his musket, his right hand parting a viewing opening through the tall grass that hid his blackened face, and along with the other soldiers of his militia company watched the Creek Indian village that belonged to the Red Stick band.

Billy nudged Alex. "Cuz, its been coming for a long time, this here morning. Remember what we were told about Fort Mimms last August, down near Mobile, Alabama. Those people didn't have much of a chance."

"Yeah. I know. The Indians that massacred those 500 militiamen, settlers, slaves, and White Stick Creeks were Red Stick's warriors. Most of them are in the camp right now below us. I heard that they took over 250 scalps that afternoon. And took 160 or more black folks as slaves."

Billy gripped his musket tighter. His hands were moist.

"Seems harsh, in a way. But they gotta pay. This army's been stomping around through the piney woods, swamps, mud, and dirt for almost a year just waiting for a chance to get even, exact a little revenge. 500 dead people, innocent settlers, kids, old people too! These here Red Stick Creeks got a payback coming!"

Alex peered through the grass. "Well, we've news for this bunch right here, right now. Hell's a coming along with shaved heads too!"

A young Creek girl gingerly lifted the edge of the hanging blanket that covered the lodge's doorway. She looked back over her shoulder at the still sleeping forms of her family, grinned slyly, and stepped out of the dwelling. A puppy lying beside the wickiup stood and licked the child's fingertips. She bent over, picked up the puppy, and hugged it to her chest. The young dog licked her chin in response. The misting fog enshrouded the Indian encampment. The girl walked quietly across the campsite, past the glowing campfire embers, constantly looking left and right to be sure that she didn't encounter an early rising adult.

Another young girl called softly to her from bushes near the gurgling branch that provided fresh water to the camp. "Moon Mist, psst, over here. Join me. We can watch the day begin before we are summoned by our parents."

Moon Mist placed her puppy on the ground between herself and her friend. The puppy jumped and pranced about, seeking the attention of the two friends.

One of the girls remarked on the other's hair and began to braid it. The child leaned back against her friend and stroked the puppy's ears. The early morning darkness was soft. The two friends and their playful pup caused the other camp dogs to relax. Now the dogs no longer formed a dependable early warning system for the Indian encampment."

The early pre-dawn darkness reflected the setting moon and still clung to the land. Alex could faintly see his cousin and other men of the company of militia that lay in ambush in the dim moonlight. Somewhere in the distance a bird call sounded shrilly. A ground fog lay across the bottom land below the small rise where Captain John Hedge waited with others of his command.

That ground fog, damp and misty, thickened. Its shrouds lurked among the wickiups of the sleeping band of Creek Indians. Not even a camp dog stirred. The fog created a quietness while the setting moon's grayness softened the early pre-dawn hour. Several glowing piles of embers from the camps fires created bright spots of reddish orange throughout the peaceful scene as a soft early breeze circulated through the camp.

The two Indian children, just like other children in other times and in other conflicts, had no reason to fear the morning.

Whispered orders were passed man to man in the American line. "Quietly, cock your musket and wait for the command."

The skyline was becoming visible. A couple of dogs stirred among the Indian shelters. One large mastiff pointed his nose toward the ridge and barked loudly. The command came, not whispered but yelled loudly.

"Charge! Charge, Men, Charge! Let none escape, no quarter! Charge! Remember Mimms. Remember Mimms, no quarter!

The first musket report shattered the dawn's stillness. A wave of running troops, some in full uniform, some in buckskins, enveloped the Indian encampment. Braves began to exit the small lodges. One massive warrior stepped into Alex's path. Alex swung his musket to knock away the Indian's firelock, twirled the musket around, and slapped the warrior's face with the gun's buttstock. The addled brave dropped to one knee! Alex brought his musket butt into his shoulder and shot the brave through the head. Blood and brain matter sprayed the lodge door's blanket covering. There was no time to reload now. Alex jerked the tomahawk from his belt and ran to the next wickiup.

One of the Red Stick's braves was standing beside the round shelter's wall, head down, attempting to charge his musket. He looked up just as Alex's sweeping swing with his belt ax almost severed the Indian's head. Bloodlust filled Alex. He ran on to the next lodging just as a woman and a young child emerged from the hut. Alex halted, startled at his arm's motion as he drew back to swing his weapon.

"Go back inside, stay there. I don't kill women!" He yelled at the woman.

She altered her path, jerked the young boy's arm, and ran toward the tree line that skirted the camp. Two militiamen stepped from the trees and fired simultaneously, dropping the woman and child into the dirt.

Alex stared, shook his head, and paused to reload his musket. He rammed the cartridge home from the muzzle down into the barrel with the ramrod, withdrew it and shoved the ramrod back into its socket thimbles, inverted the gun, charged the pan, dropped the frizzen, cocked the hammer, and ran into the center of the encampment. A Creek warrior was leaning over a short log palisade preparing to fire toward the charging infantry. Alex swung the musket into his shoulder, aimed hastily, and put a ball into the brave, knocking him down.

The camp was beginning to burn. The light from the fires and muzzle flashes among the lodges created a lurid spectacle as the running Indians and charging soldiers clashed. Most of the fighting now was hand to hand, with knives, belt axes or tomahawks, along with an occasional pistol's discharge. An arrow whizzed by Alex's head. Instinctively, he ducked and turned to his right, searching for the foe. The Indian dropped his bow, useless now with no arrows remaining in his quiver. He charged

Alex, bowled him over with his shoulder, and dropped on top of him.

Alex grasped for his tomahawk and slapped the ground empty-handed. The Indian had his forearm pressed against Alex's jugular.....that's when Alex fingers found the shaft of his hawk, grasped it, and swung as hard as he could upward. The tomahawk blade stuck the Indian between his shoulder and neck. The enemy momentarily released his hold on Alex, allowing him another swing, this one better aimed. He buried the weapon's blade into the enemy's forehead just above the bridge of his nose. Alex pushed the bleeding corpse off of his chest and stood up, then jerked the tomahawk from the still-quivering Indian's skull.

The fight between the company of militia and the hostile Creeks was winding down. Short and violent in intensity, the encampment area now was strangely silent, almost serene. Some of the older militia troops were going from body to body, tracing their skinning knives around the skulls, and then grabbing a handful of hair, slamming a foot on the enemy's neck and jerking the scalp from the still forms of the fallen foe.

A small band of Creek Indian survivors, mostly the aged, as well as women and children, were being herded at gunpoint into a group in the center of the village near the larger lodge. Alex spotted the two young girls from the brook standing at the outer edge of the group. The puppy was still frisking about when suddenly it was booted out of the way by one of the militia guardsmen.

An Indian woman in a buckskin skirt gestured to the two girls. Alex noticed that the woman's buckskin mantle had wisps of human hair dangling as ornaments from the bodice. "Scalp locks!" He muttered to himself. "We aren't the only bloody-minded people about."

Alex flinched as an arm was suddenly draped around his shoulders.

"We showed them this time, didn't we, Alexander? Suppose they ken expect to leave us Scots be from now onward, what say!" Corporal Richard Coburn grinned as he brushed some of the blood and debris of the battle from his face. "Blood for Blood, me Pa always said."

The Indian woman screamed in defiance as a soldier pushed her back into the group of captives. Both men saw the wisps of hair on the woman's garments.

Coburn nudged Alex. "I suspect those be scalp locks from some of their victims of the Fort Mimms massacre, what? Maybe, just maybe, we've evened the score somewhat. Maybe give her a bit of the taste of what these Injuns did to our folks at Mimms, ay."

Alex brushed away the Corporal's arm. His mind was still confused with the bloody fight's aftermath. He spoke sharply to the bellicose braggart. "I've had enough blood for one day, enough killing. I'd think that you would have too, if you weren't such a posturing bastert! Go praise yourself to someone else, just get the hell away from me!"

The earlier order given at the time of the charge command had been no quarter. Any surviving Creek warriors remaining from Red Stick's followers were immediately executed, either by a quick musket shot or a knife plunged into the heart of the captive along with the cry "Remember Fort Mimms".

None survived outside a small group of women and children along with the aged Indians held captive by the encircling military guardsmen.

CHAPTER TWO

Billy Rudd

Three days later the militia regiment reached the natural ford on the Ocmulgee River that fronted Fort Hawkins and crossed over to the settlement of Macon, Georgia, making camp on the broad parade ground that fronted the frontier post.

The troops were weary. They had won a major battle and marched a straight three days afterward and brought their prisoners to Fort Hawkins. Now for the first time in over a week Alex pulled his boots off and lay stretched out in front of a roaring fire, relaxing in its warmth and wiggling his toes in dirty mended stockings. He fell asleep.

Alex's warm slumber was interrupted by someone seating himself beside him.

"Hey Cuz! You awake?" Billy Rudd asked.

"I guess I am now." Alex grunted in frustration as his napping was interrupted.

"You know, Alex, that it's rumored that Ol Hickory, 'Andy by God' Jackson himself is supposed to be here possibly tomorrow."

"No, I hadn't heard anything bout that, Billy."

"I heard talk of it over at the mess tent about an hour ago. Seems that General Jackson is preparing an armed force to march down to New Orleans and secure the port just in case the Bloody Britishers were to show up with a fleet. He had called on Colonel Nash to help by us joining his force. What'cha think about that?"

"I think that's a little over 500 miles more of marching. And I'm tired and footsore. We've walked a long way, you and I; you since coming from South Carolina, over near Pendleton and me from Kingston. We've wandered all over Georgia from our Carolina foothills almost to the coast and back to the mountains, now down here to Hawkins. I've about had enough walking and I want my horse back now. Or just any good horse."

Billy stretched his hands toward the fire. "You know the Captain ain't gonna let you ride when the rest of the company is walking. So, what you gonna do; desert!"

Alex was quiet and stared at the fire for a few moments. "I guess!"

Billy twisted around and squinted at his cousin. "We've come a far piece, that's true. But you know, they shoot deserters, or at least brand them with a big D on their cheek. You want that?"

"Not particularly. But I've been in this army long enough. I've done my part and I've seen the elephant, seen battle. Now I want to see that big river that I keep hearing about. Our Indian allies said it was the Father of all Rivers, they called it Miss-iss-ippi. They say it is as wide as a half day's march is long."

"I swear, Alex, sounds as if you've caught a case of Alabama Fever in this desire to see sights you've only heard tell of."

"That's how come I'm here now, Billy Rudd. I heard tell of a march against some Indians that had burned a fort in Georgia, remember, Fort Mimms...and you must have too, cause here we both sit on the banks of a muddy river in the middle of Georgia trying to erase our visions of death and violence, all the horror of this bloody warfare."

Billy scratched his head. "What about the folks back at our homes. You've got people down near the coast at Kingston Town and my family is on the old homestead farm near the village of Pendleton. You plan on going back?"

"No, I think not. I've worked enough on that farm. My kin were aware when I left that I probably wouldn't return. I thought then that West seems like a good direction to travel and explore, especially since our country has all this new land that we've gained after the Revolutionary War and then this new purchase from the French that some are calling Louisiana. Besides, I wrote my sister and her husband a letter last month. Told them what I was doing and that I was thinking about cutting loose and heading on toward the West."

"I see your point, Alex. Hadn't thought about it before. Nothing for me back on the farm either but work." Both men were silent until Billy spoke out again. "Listen Alex, if, just if I was so inclined, would you help me write a letter to my folks. I think I'd like to go along with you, that is if'n you wouldn't mind the company."

Alex nodded in the affirmative. "Sounds feasible to me. I'll help with your letter. We will need to find some horses tomorrow before some officer decides to march us somewhere. We're gonna need some better rifles than these muskets too. I've got a bit of cash. You have any?"

Billy grinned. "I can find some in my pack. I guess I'm going on a trek along with you then!"

Alex pulled his blanket up to his chin, rolled over, and placed his back toward the fire. "Find your bedroll. I'm gonna find us mounts right after daylight. Then we'll write your letter to your homefolks. Let's get some shuteye now."

CHAPTER THREE

Lieutenant Preston Winston Francine

The foot log spanned the narrow creek. Alex crossed first with Billy following close behind. The two young men topped a rise just beyond the creek and stood at the edge of a plowed field.

A clapboard cabin nestled between two oak trees three hundred yards distant.

"This must be the place." Alex muttered.

"What place? This be where we've been going all morning? I thought that we were seeking horses." Billy grumbled.

"Our regiment's White Stick Creek scout said a man named Mercer had a farm close by. The Indian said he raised horses and mules. From what he described this looks right."

Alex stepped out of the tree line and into the open. "Halloooo, the cabin. Hallooo." He yelled and started walking toward the dwelling.

"Well kept farm." Billy muttered. "Must belong to a white man from the looks of the work on the place."

"I doubt it, Billy. The Creek said that Mercer was a mixed breed. Half Scot and half Cherokee. I 'spect we'll know in a minute." Alex halted and called out again. The two men watched the cabin door swing open. A man stepped from the log dwelling and motioned them onward.

The man standing in front of the cabin's door was average height with long loosely flowing hair. He was dressed in buckskin leggings, moccasins, and a large blue flannel shirt. Two flintlock pistols were tucked into a flaming scarlet sash that adorned his waist. "Mercer's my name. Jock Mercer. Jest what do ye call yourselves."

"I'm Alex Avery. And my companion is Billy Rudd. We're traveling about from South Carolina and need to purchase some horses. I was advised that you might have some for sale. Any truth in that?"

"Avery and Rudd. Be ye lads Scottish, by chance?"

Billy answered first. "Probably so, at least in the past families."

Mercer grinned. "Then, yes, I raise horses. You'uns looking for riding stock or work horses?"

"We're traveling west toward the new lands. So, we need riding stock, two at least and a couple more broke enough to carry packs." Alex rested his musket butt on the ground.

Jock Mercer stepped down from the cabin's door stoop and started toward a corral behind the house. "Well, come on and let's see if you like any of my stock. Two horses gonna cost you 50 dollars each, no Continentals! Pack animals broken about 30 dollars each."

Billy grimaced. "Being a Carolina farm boy, that seems a mite high. We'll give you a hundred dollars in gold for four animals, aye, and not a penny more."

"In gold, you say." Mercer wet his lips. "You must be Scots. You started dickering before my words chilled."

Billy nodded. "Aye, Jocko, in gold coin. We'll throw in another 20 for two good saddles, blankets, bridals, and pack frames. Have we a deal?"

"We do. Those six in the corral are saddle wise. Pick the pair that you want. I've two pack horses in the barn. Just fed them. You didn't ask but I'll throw in a sack of grain for feed as well." Mercer held his hand out toward Billy. They shook hands.

Billy waited until Mercer entered the barn and then counted out two dozen $ 5.00 gold coins from his pack. "Cuz, I'll pay for the mounts, you buy our arms when its time."

Mercer returned leading two horses, a sturdy bay and a black. Each bore pack saddles with a grain bag secured in place.

Billy counted out 24 capped bust liberty U.S. 5.00 shiny gold coins into Mercer's palm and the deal was made.

Alex got a lead rope on the two chosen saddle mounts, a grey and a buckskin and tethered them to a top rail of the corral. Mercer carried two saddles and saddle blankets down from the barn. He had two sets of reins and bridles thrown over his shoulder. Alex thanked him and set about saddling the horses.

Alex and Billy, mounted now, headed West leading their pack horses, with their muskets slung from their shoulders.

"Feels good to ride again instead of walking." Alex looked over at his cousin.

Billy nodded. "Wonder how long it'll take before we're missed."

"Probably several days or more. At least until the next muster. See here, we can't be too far away from the ford of the Ocmulgee River. That's four miles from Ft. Hawkings. There's a trading post at the ford. Let's see if we can gather our supplies there. We could get back across the river this afternoon and travel for a ways west toward Fort Mitchell on the Chattahoochee River before dark. Sort of distance ourselves from Colonel Nash's army and Fort Hawkins. It'll take several days riding to get to Ft. Mitchell. It's about 120 miles or so. What do you think?" Alex asked.

Billy nodded yes, spurred the buckskin, and the duo loped towards the outpost on the Ocmulgee Ford.

The oilskin window covering didn't allow much light into the log building that served as a store and a saloon. After their eyes adjusted to the gloom, Alex and Billy could make out the saloon's bar, just a wide wooden plank resting on two hogshead barrels, and the four board tables that fronted the remainder of the room. Several men were playing cards at one table while two soldiers, one a lieutenant and the other a corporal leaned against the bar, savoring their cups of Kentucky distilled whiskey.

A short fat florid man wearing a bartender's apron approached Alex and Billy. "Drinks are over here if'n you're thirsty. Two bits a shot, one for the whiskey and one for the cup....that's for me washing the cup."

"We're not thirsty. Just needing some supplies. Like to buy a couple of slabs of bacon and some things." Alex said.

The bartender pointed toward the window. "Supplies in that room over there. Be there in a minute."

Alex noticed the half dozen long rifles on a rack behind the store's counter. His buckskin leggings whispered against the floor's planking as he moved closer to view the guns. Billy moved over beside him. The fat florid trader scurried behind the counter. "You boys have a list of what you need?"

"No, not written. I'll tell you though. You can start the bill with 5 pounds of flour and a side of bacon. And if you have a tin or two of crackers and two pounds of coffee, that'll be good too." Alex said in a low voice. The storekeeper began to pile the supplies onto the counter.

Billy waited for a moment. "And a twist of tobacco, no, make that two, and a bag of those trade beads over there, the red and blue ones."

Alex continued. "Two flannel shirts hanging there behind you and let me look at the two long rifles sitting on the left end of the rack, please."

"You men got the means to pay for all this. You look like you're traveling a bit light."

Alex stood straight, his six-foot height towering over the stumpy man. "Sir, with all respect to you, I find that question rude. If I couldn't afford the supplies, I wouldn't be in here. Now, if that brings satisfaction to your arrogant question, I'd like to see those two rifles. And while you're over there, bring those two flintlock pistols lying on the counter in front of them. Now is fine." Alex's tone was flat, filled with polite menace.

The trader gently laid the two rifles on the counter. Alex picked the rifle with a darker hued wood up and swung the curly maple stock into his shoulder and turned, pointing at the oilskin window. The silver blade front sight on the flintlock's long octagonal barrel glinted against the little light emitted through the window. The gunmaker's name was clearly etched on the barrel flat, Frederick Zorger. Alex dropped the stock from his shoulder and rested the rifle in his right hand, palm up and opened. The rifle lay perfectly aligned and even, resting smoothly in his hand. Alex opened the frizzen and drew the hammer to full cock, set the rear trigger with his forefinger, and held the cocked hammer with his left hand while pulling the front trigger to check the weight and feel the drop of the hammer. He rested the curved buttplate on his boot and felt the muzzle with his finger tip, mentally counting the rifling cuts and feeling of their crispness.

"That's a 40 caliber bore out of York, Pennsylvania," stated the clerk. The other one on the counter is a Pennypacker, Daniel Pennypacker, also out of Pennsylvania. It's a .50 caliber. I've had them for less than a year. Both guns are well kept. Cheaper if you buy them both."

Alex looked at Billy and spoke quietly. "Check out the drop and feel of the Pennypacker. See if it fits you. The barrel looks a mite longer, maybe two inches, likely due to the caliber increase. Billy nodded and picked the rifle up and examined it much in the same manner as his cousin had the Zorger gun.

"Muzzle and rifling don't appear worn, action is crisp. Looks good to me, Alex."

Alex leaned down to the clerk's height and looked him directly in the eyes. "How much for both? Be careful of your price as we aren't finished yet. And while you are tossing the price about in your mind, let me see those two Carolina pistols."

The florid fat clerk dutifully handed the pistols over to Alex. Alex looked the two belt guns over. "Definitely Carolina guns," he thought. Both handguns bore the mark of Joseph Mordecai. "Look, Cuz. These two handguns were made by a gunsmith out of Charleston, South Carolina. I was in his shop on Liberty Street just four years past. He knows his trade." He looked at the clerk. "I'll take these as well. Now, name your price!"

The clerk wiped his face with the dingy bar towel. "Well, about...."

"Careful, now, clerkie boy," Billy muttered.

The clerk stammered. "I was gonna ask 20.00 dollars each for the rifles, but since you're buying the pistols too, I'll throw them into the bargain, say $50.00 dollars for all four.... Along with some spare flints and a powder horn for each rifle."

Alex rubbed his nose. "We'll need some accoutrements. The necessary bullet molds for each gun. Since the pistols are in .50 caliber, we need two 50 caliber molds and one .40 for the rifle., a couple of touch hole picks, and a rifleman's parts tool. Do that and you have a deal. Hard cash too!"

The clerk nodded.

Alex continued to speak. "Put 35 pounds of bullet lead on the counter, two shelter halves, and 3 quarter kegs of gunpowder, rifle powder sized, it'll work for all the gun bores, don'tcha know. And, add in one quarter keg of priming powder. And half a yard of linen for patching. Oh, and a sack of beans. Let's see now, add us about 10 pounds of shelled corn and a flint and steel fire starter. Total it up while I go retrieve your payment. Watch him, Billy, make sure he gets the order right. And if you want, add a couple of broad brimmed hats to the order. They'll help in the coming weeks of spring weather."

Billy nodded agreement. He picked up one of the Carolina pistols, drew his belt knife, and cut two small strips of the linen material from the goods piled on the counter. He poured a measure of powder from the horn slung over his shoulder into the gun's muzzle. Then he spit on one of the two linen patches and placed it over the muzzle's opening. Withdrawing a lead ball from his belt pouch, Billy pushed the ball down into the damp patch and into the muzzle. He watched the clerk intently as he withdrew the pistol's ramrod and used it to shove the patched ball down the gun's barrel. The fat clerk kept glancing over his shoulder almost like Billy might be a threat.

The Army Lieutenant shoved himself erect from his lounging position against the plank bar and staggered to the trading post door. Handsome, in a soft, smooth faced way with shaggy blonde hair and soft blue eyes, Lieutenant Preston Winston Francine watched as Alex removed a leather pouch from the pack of the bay horse tethered beside the tall gray stud.

Alex stepped up onto the trading post's porch and entered the doorway, bumping Francine.

"Excuse me, Sir, didn't see you there in the gloom." Alex strode to the store's counter and the waiting clerk. "You have a total for all the goods now?"

"With the guns, clothing, and general supplies, I tallied it up at 117.00 dollars." The clerk stammered nervously.

"Add two jugs of Kentucky distilled spirits and I'll give you $120.00 in hard coin." Alex shook the leather poke, jingling the coins inside, and the clerk nodded as he hurried off to fetch the liquor. While he was gone, Alex counted out 5 gold U.S. quarter eagles and 95 silver Spanish Milled Dollars and pushed them into a pile on the counter. By the time that the clerk had removed the pile of coins and stored them behind the counter, Billy had carried the supplies and the guns out to the porch and was loading them on the pack horses.

Alex joined him and together they finished packing the two horses and lashing oiled canvas tarps down over the supplies.

Lieutenant Francine moved to the porch and leaned against the roof support. The Lieutenant watched as Alex and Billy loaded their new long rifles and charged the pans, then loaded the Carolina belt pistols.

The corporal joined Francine on the porch just as Alex turned around and faced the two soldiers. Alex's eyes widened, then narrowed slightly in surprise. The second soldier was none other than Corporal Richard Coburn of Alex's former company!

Lieutenant Francine grinned slyly. "You two boys look like you might be planning a trip, say, away from Fort Hawkins. I don't think that Colonel Nash or the U.S. Army will think much of that idea. But, not having been discharged from the U-nited S-tates Army you wouldn't be doing that, would you?" The lieutenant burped behind his hand.

Billy barked back, "Mister, I'm not in your army right now. And my pardner's not either!"

Francine growled. "The hell you say. Those white britches tucked into your boots are army issue, now aren't they!

Your pardner had enough sense to change his to buckskins, but I bet he's from Nash's South Carolina Volunteers just like you are!"

"He is, he is! That's the Carolina soldier that fought alongside us in my company five days ago before we marched to Hawkins. And, Lieutenant, I know that man, Lieutenant! I spoke with him right after the Red Sticks, what was left of them, surrendered. He's definitely a soldier now just like he was last week! But where they going with them horses and all that gear?"

Lieutenant Francine grinned broadly. "I'm going to issue you two soldiers an order this very minute. You can keep your supplies, but you take those horses to the quartermaster at Fort Hawkins and turn them in! You are not cavalry, you're infantry! And right now, I think you are planning to desert!" He chuckled. "Tell you what though. I have an idea. Corporal, you go back inside and have that fat barkeep pour you and me another drink cause I'm buying. I'll be there in a minute to pay him!"

Coburn did a drunken about face accompanied by a sloppy salute and staggered back to the bar.

"Travelers are you? Not likely. Sounds to me that you just might like to back up your lies with some coin, maybe enough to make me want to turn around and go back into the bar while you consider your departure. Well, tell you what, Private or Mister traveler or whatever you are;" Francine belched loudly. "That was a pile of silver and gold you placed on that counter in there. You've still got the poke, I suspect. And it still looked sort of plump when you put it away. Tell you what, give me the poke and I'll go back into the bar for a couple of hours while you make your getaway.... Since your partner says you and he ain't army, you don't have much to worry about if the Corporal and I don't let on. So how about it? Why not just hand over the poke!"

Alex stepped onto the porch. "Okay." Alex poked the muzzle of his rifle hard into the Lieutenant's stomach and then flipped the butt of the new Kentucky rifle around toward the

Lieutenant and jabbed it sharply between the man's legs into his groin. The lieutenant's knees buckled, he gagged and started to pitch forward. Alex butt-stroked him again under his jaw and watched as the man slammed backwards, his head striking the porch post. He switched the rifle to his left hand and jerked his tomahawk from his belt. He was in the act of raising it for a striking blow at the fallen officer when Billy grabbed his arm.

"Don't! Not now, cuz. He's down. You don't want to kill him. That would give the army a reason to chase us! The first two blows rendered him unconscious instantly."

Alex quickly examined the wrist and butt of his new rifle. It was unbroken. He looked at Francine. "There's the only poke you'll get from me, Lieutenant. Hope you enjoy your earnings! You asked for it! Let's ride, Billy."

Alex swung into the grey's saddle and laid heels to his flank. Together he and Billy Rudd cantered toward the Ocmulgee River's ford and led their pack horses on west toward the new territory.

Meanwhile, back at Fort Hawkins, Captain John Hedge stretched his back and groaned. He had been sitting at his camp desk too long.

"Sergeant Long!" The captain yelled.

"Sir!" The sergeant faced the desk and saluted.

"Sergeant Long, didn't you detail someone to go to the Ocmulgee trading post for some coffee beans, some other supplies, and a jug of stump water?"

"Sir, I did. Lieutenant Francine was to check on our men in the infirmary. Afterward he was going into the settlement and the trader's. I detailed Corporal Coburn to accompany him. They should have been back by now, Sir!"

"As you can see, Sergeant, they are not! Form a detail and go find them and report back to me, with the Lieutenant and the coffee beans! Best take a wagon for transport. They may have encountered a problem. Be quick! And don't forget the Stump Water!"

"Sir!" And the sergeant hurried from the tent.

Corporal Richard Coburn downed the cup of whiskey that the bartender had placed in front of him, hicupped loudly, and turned to face the card players.

"Wonder what's keeping the Lieutenant." Coburn muttered. He turned back toward the bartender. "Pour me another one while I'm waiting, Please good sir." The corporal slurred his words, turned, and staggered over to the card players' table. He peered over the shoulder of one. "Nice hand, mister." Coburn whispered loudly. "Nice hand."

The card player laid his cards face down on the table, stood, and shoved the drunken soldier away and back toward the bar. "Go finish your drinking, boy, and leave us be."

Coburn turned and came back toward the gamblers. This time he staggered around the table and stood behind another player. He whispered loudly over the man's head while looking at the first player across the table, "He's got two Aces, he does now! And a couple of ladies too!"

Before the words were in the air good, the first card player drew a pistol from his belt, leveled it at the drunken soldier, and pulled the trigger. The flash from the heavy caliber gun lit the gloomy room for an instant. A bloody splotch appeared on Corporal Coburn's waistcoat below and to the left of his chin. Richard Coburn looked down at his chest and up at the shooter.

"Hell's bells, you've killed me!" Coburn said and fell over dead.

The card players cleared the cash from the table. One said to the others, "Time to go!" And they headed for the door, dashing past the unconscious Lieutenant who lay on the porch of the trading post.

Sergeant Long stopped the wagon team at the front of the command tent. He jumped down from the wagon seat and dragged the still unsteady Lieutenant Francine from the wagon. He held the junior officer upright and marched him into the tent, halting the two prescribed steps from the Company Commander's desk.

"Sir, Captain Hedge, Sir!" Sergeant Long released the Lieutenant's arm and attempted a salute, turning quickly to support the still wobbly Lieutenant Francine.

"Sir, I found the Lieutenant. But Corporal Coburn's body is stretched out in the wagon bed, Sir."

The captain stood up and faced Sergeant Long and the disheveled Lieutenant. "What's the meaning of this, Lieutenant Francine?" The Lieutenant attempted to salute and leaned against the sergeant.

"Sergeant," the Captain spoke sharply, "Step away from the Lieutenant. He can stand alone or fall down! Lieutenant, you are a disgrace. Account for yourself. Are you drunk? And on duty?"

"Captain, Sir. I would like to report a deserter, Sir. I found him in the trading post, Sir. It was two of them, Sir. Two, and one of them wore army britches, Sir. They had horses, too, and were buying supplies." Francine's words were slurred.

"And I'm not drunk sir. I only had one cup full of the juice of the corn to quench my thirst sir, after the walk to the settlement. That's when I saw the deserters that I'm reporting, Captain. I only paused long enough to assure myself that the Stump Water would be to your liking. Corporal Coburn was with me, and he saw them too. The two deserters. Yes, he did! And I need the Provost Guard to go and arrest them Sir."

"Lieutenant," Captain Hedge growled, "You're a disgrace to your uniform! Your pants are torn, you've blood on your shirt collar, you face is bruised and bloody, your scalp is torn, and your eye is blackening. And you stink. You smell of cheap corn whiskey."

"But Sir, the deserters.", Lieutenant Francine wailed.

The Captain glanced over at the Sergeant. "Long, go get Corporal Coburn out of the wagon. I want to hear his version. Wake him up if he's drunk too!"

"Sir, I can't wake Coburn up, Sir."

"Pray tell, Sergeant, just why not!"

"Cause Coburn's dead, sir."

"Dead, you say!" Captain Hedge shouted. "How in thunder did the corporal get dead! More deserters?"

"Sir, best I can tell from the accounts I heard, Captain, some card players shot him because he was drunk and interrupted their poker game!" Sergeant Long shifted his body stance to that of parade rest but still looked straight ahead.

Captain Hedge addressed Sergeant Long. "Just where was the Lieutenant while Coburn was getting himself shot and killed?"

Francine attempted to answer before Sergeant Long could.

"Captain, I was attempting to halt and arrest the two deserters when they attacked and jumped me!"

"Is that the truth, Sergeant. Speak up now!" Hedge spoke stridently.

"Doubtful, Sir. But I really don't know. The Lieutenant was unconscious and lying on the porch outside of the trading post when I got there. He smelled real strong too, Sir."

"Lieutenant Francine interrupted again. "Captain, Sir, we've got to go after those two deserters, Sir. They could be getting away now."

"Lieutenant Francine. Your performance gives me concern for your future in the United States Army. You are in a disgraceful state, Sir. And your actions leave me no choice but to discipline you. And, if you think that for even a minute I'll buy into your story about two deserters taking French Leave, then you are sadly mistaken! I've got over 50 wounded men in camp from that affair with Red Stick's savages only three days past as well as a dozen or more unaccounted-for soldiers that are probably dead within the forest surrounding that encampment we attacked. And you think that I could identify two deserters on the words of a drunken slovenly officer and a dead corporal!" The captain walked over to the Lieutenant and leaned close to his face, wrinkling his nose against the man's drunken smell.

"I'm sentencing you to 60 days in the Fort Hawkins jail. And daily, you will serve your sentence by working at cleaning the latrines or sinks and carrying the slops from the barracks. This time, and only because you are an officer and declared a gentleman by an act of Congress, you can retain your rank....but your pay for those two months will be denied. Sergeant, get this disgusting excuse of an officer out of my sight and over to the guardhouse. And dump whatever remains of Corporal Coburn off at the infirmary for the medics to inspect and prepare for burial. Dismissed!"

CHAPTER FOUR

Tobias Walking Horse

Several months passed. The cousins took their time and explored the lands where they rode. In time they neared Fort Mitchell in the new Alabama territory bordering the state of Georgia's west boundary. Fort Mitchell was bustling with new settlers. Alex and Billy felt like they should travel farther west in search of a permanent homestead after encountering so many people.

"Less people, more opportunity for land."Alex said over and over. They had spent the night in the sleeping loft of the Elk Horn tavern and trading post at Fort Mitchell. Next morning following their breakfast, they loaded their pack animals, and had just saddled their mounts when a heavy-set man grabbed Billy's shoulder, spun him around, and slashed at him with a large bladed belt knife. Billy attempted to dodge away from the attack but the knife blade sliced his face from his ear lobe down his jaw to his chin.

His attacker yelled in anger. "You lily livered cur, you'll bleed for this. I've been wondering when you'ld show your face around these parts again. You put a bullet through my pardner when his back was turned, coward!"

Alex turned and drew his pistol, cocking the hammer with his off hand, and leveling the belt gun toward the stranger's face.

"Freeze, basterd, or die! Freeze now, and not another step ere it will be your last!" Alex moved to Billy's side and handed him his neckerchief. "Cover the wound, quickly now." The pistol never waivered and Alex never took his eyes off the attacker. "Other than the cut to your face, did he get you anywhere else, Billy?"

"No, only my face. He wasn't quick enough, or you were faster on the draw."

The attacker sprang toward the two men, launching another attack. Alex's pistol roared. The muzzle flash was so close that the stranger's beard erupted into flame as his head was thrown back from the impact of the pistol ball. The attacker collapsed to the ground, dead. Alex calmly pulled the pistol's ramrod, poured a measure of powder down the barrel, and pressed a lead ball from his bullet pouch down the barrel atop the powder charge, opened the frizzen, and charged the pan. After snapping the frizzen firmly down on the pan, he holstered the loaded pistol and stood beside Billy, ready, wary, watching the street.

Another stranger loomed up beside Alex. "That was some quick reaction, young fella. Ol' Donavan had it coming. Had to happen sooner or later. Anytime that he got into his cups and saw a stranger, he'd try to pick a fight. This time his victim didn't run!" And he slapped Alex on the back. "Well done, well done. Let's see about getting your companion cleaned and doctored up. We've a makeshift sawbones in the shanty next door. This early in the day, he's bound to be sober. Come along."

Several hours later after Billy's wound was cleansed and stitched, the cousins retrieved their pack animals, mounted their horses, and rode out of Fort Mitchell heading northwest. They rode slow, favoring the pain of Billy's facial wound, and savoring the wilderness that immediately surrounded them. The forest's floor was clear of underbrush due to the thickness of the timber. Pine, spruce, oak, hickory, and elm trees created a canopy that prevented undergrowth. Laurel and rhododendron grew abundantly along the forest edges and near the streams. It was awesome, new, fresh, and beckoning to the pair of wanderers.

They rode easy, letting their mounts slowly pick their way through the forested terrain. In so doing they left a trail that a blind man could follow.

The Cherokee brave watched the two riders with their pack animals as they passed beneath the rocky ledge where he lay hidden. As soon as they passed, he slid down from the rocks, retrieved his horse, swung up onto its back, and picked up their trail. He followed slowly, refraining from breaking cover, often riding above the trail where they rode, or dropping down to the stream beds alongside their passage way, but following, listening occasionally to the banter and laughter of the two cousins when he would draw near.

The sun set and shadows enveloped the forest. Billy and Alex found a clearing near a small mountain stream that afforded fresh water and made camp just before dark. Unknown to them, they had crossed into the lands described by the Georgia State Government as the Indian Territories. In the distance they could see the crest of a mountain. After letting the horses drink, the two men hobbled the animals, built a small fire, spread their bedrolls against a fallen hickory log, and prepared their meal of bacon and coffee.

Billy tenderly touched his bandaged face. "Gonna be marked for life now. My rugged handsomeness is gone forever."

Alex laughed and pointed at his cousin's face. "Once it heals, Billy Boy, if you're past your tender years, simply grow a beard. No one'll ever know what lies beneath. And you can still imagine that you're handsome!"

"Alex, you are the soul of compassion. I am suitably impressed with your thoughtfulness."

Alex stood and carried a lariat over to his hobbled horse, threaded one end to the horse's halter, and came back to his bedroll, letting the lariat drag out on the ground. He tied the rope's end around his left wrist, drew his tomahawk from his belt, and stretched out on his blankets, resting his back against his saddle that lay next to the fallen tree. The warmth from the fire was soothing. His muscles ached. He looked over at Billy.

"You might want to drop a rope over your horse, Cuz. Maybe tie one end to your saddle. Hate for a panther or some other critter to stampede our stock and leave us afoot in the morning. Nite!" Alex was asleep before Billy returned to his blankets.

Long about first light, Alex was suddenly awakened when his arm was jerked hard by his frightened horse. He grasped the rope that was secured to his left wrist and stood up just as a human form stepped out of the darkness beneath the trees.

"Hello, the camp! My name is Tobias Walking Horse. I am alone. Can I come to the fire?"

Billy spoke first. "If you are a friend and not a foe, approach slowly with your hands out." He looked over at Alex. "You armed, Cuz?" Alex nodded yes.

The Indian approached the campfire as Alex kicked a log onto the hot embers, creating more light and a profusion of sparks.

Tobias dropped his horse's reins. The animal, ground broke, stood fast. Tobias walked toward the fire with his hands stretched out in front, empty palms up.

The Indian was of average height, lean and muscular. He wore his hair in a tall scalp lock, adorned with a turkey feather that dangled from the back of his head. Each side of his face was adorned with nine circular tattoos, and a copper earring hung from his right ear lobe.

A mantle made of rabbit and ermine furs draped his shoulders, fur side worn inward to ward off the night chill. A buckskin breechclout topped his fringed leggings that ended in calf high moccasins. A snakeskin belt encircled the man's waist, supporting his legging strings, breechclout, and a long sheathed knife. A possibles bag was suspended on his left side. A beaded quiver holding three arrows and a slender bow hung across his back.

Astonished, Billy involuntarily covered his mouth with his hand when the Indian stepped into the firelight.

Still on guard, Alex held his handgun muzzle down, finger still resting on the trigger.

"Speak your piece! Why do you follow us?"

Tobias Walking Horse motioned northward. "You are traveling North. You seem to have little concern for the lands or this wilderness that surrounds you. Two white men, mounted on horses, leading pack animals....create a fine target for defeated Red Stick warriors, those who have followed northern Indian Chief Tecumseh. Me, I White Stick, many of us of South, of lower Creek villages, followed Alex McGillivary. "I Cherokee, had Creek wife and child. Lost them in a raid on my village. For time before war started, we lived near trading post. Given name Tobias there."

Alex felt some of the tension easing. "So, why do you follow us if we appear harmless?"

Tobias nodded. "You are strangers to the area. I wish to travel north also, but fear odds against one, me!. If I could go with you, be much safer for all three as party is larger."

Alex tucked his pistol into his holster after uncocking it. "Sounds reasonable. How are you outfitted?"

The Indian nodded. "I am horsed, have bow and knife, some dried meat and berries, pemican. No musket, powder, or ball. Horse not gaunt. Feet are good.

So, what say you, white man?"

Alex looked over the fire at the now relaxed Billy. Billy nodded yes. Alex offered his hand to the Indian. Tobias clasped Alex's hand and their eyes met in agreement.

"We are traveling toward the Miss-iss-ipp-i, the big river. We wish to explore the land and maybe go beyond the big water." Alex turned toward Billy. "Cuz, brew up some coffee. We need to do some planning." He turned back as Tobias spoke.

"Father of Waters, this Miss-iss-ipp-i. I have not seen it, only heard stories of its vastness and the great and rich hunting lands that border the river. I have no family now after the British and Red Stick war on my people. I can go along, too?"

Alex nodded affirmatively. "Notice that you only have three remaining arrows. If we are to be traveling together, you will need better arms. Have ye fired a musket before?....And do you know how to load the arm?"

The Indian nodded yes. "I can use and load. Lost mine several moons back and have not found another."

"I have a spare musket and powder, horn, and ball. I can give it now and you can trade me something later. Agreed?"

"Yes. I have noticed you wear a Cherokee tomahawk. I have heard the campfire talk of a white man from the coast of Carolina who fights fiercely with the hatchet...Are you that man?"

"Might be. Don't know. The hatchet was my fathers from long ago in the war with the red coated soldiers. But yes, I have fought enemies with that weapon, the one of which you speak."

The sun had risen. The three men, having shared coffee, breakfast, and the beginning of trust, mounted and rode northwest.

CHAPTER FIVE

Poinsettia Posey Vaughn

Poinsettia "Posey" Vaughn pulled herself up to a standing position using the rear of the wagon seat and leaned forward. "Momma, can I get out of the wagon. I need to be excused."

Julie Vaughn smiled at her older daughter. Nearing 11 years now, it seemed that it was only yesterday when she was born in Charleston and named for Julie's favorite cousin Joel Poinsett and his favored plant the Poinsettia. Posey's childhood awkwardness was disappearing, and her speech was more concise, more adult in content and expression. Julie reined in the team of mules at the edge of a small forest meadow. "Take your little sister Mona with you. That way we won't have to stop again for a spell. Hurry along, now, the two of you."

Posey tugged at her sister Monique. "You heard Mama. Come on, Mona. Let's go. The grass and everything looks so clean here." The two girls Posey, and Mona, age 7, climbed out of the wagon bed and scampered across the clearing to a large fallen log. They climbed over it and made themselves comfortable. Afterward, Mona crawled across the mossy ground toward the uprooted tree's roots and picked a handful of buttercups. Posey joined her. The two young girls huddled together, just enjoying the morning moment and being sisters.

Posey watched as her father rode out of the forest and up to the wagon.

"Julie," he called, I'm going on ahead for a quarter mile or so. As soon as the girls have stretched their legs, get them back in the wagon and come on to me. Don't linger too long. Others have crossed this trail recently."

Posey stretched out on the soft green moss, enjoying the sunlight that filtered through the trees. Her mother's shrieking scream startled her. She peered over the log and watched as her mother attempted to pull an arrow from the small of her back, failed in the attempt, and fell from the wagon seat.

Three savages ran from the forest at the rear of the wagon. One ran to the prone woman, placed his foot on her neck, and ran a scalping knife around her hairline, yanked upward, and tore Julie's long braided hair from her skull; shook the fresh scalp in the air, and screamed a war cry.

Posey lunged for her sister Mona, covering her body with her own and whispered harshly, "Indians! They've killed Moma. Lay still under me, be very quiet. They must not know we are here. Whatever happens, don't make a sound!" Mona nodded.

Julie's husband John had heard his wife scream. Two of the three Indians heard his horse coming hard through the trees and rushed to each side of the trail just as the rider and his mount came into the meadow. One of the braves launched an arrow that struck John in the neck. The other warrior jumped to the horse's head and grabbed its halter, turned, and sank his tomahawk into the rider's chest. The man tumbled from the saddle. The Indian that scalped John's wife ran to the fallen man with his drawn scalping knife and quickly added a second scalp to his grisly collection. One of the warriors mounted the horse and the two others followed him up the forest trail after retrieving the musket that John Vaughn had carried.

The two children hugged each other tightly, frightened, but lying still, hoping to be overlooked by the marauders. Minutes passed. After a time of stillness, Posey peeked over the log.

Her mother's body lay where she had fallen. Her father John lay near the mule team. John moaned softly.

"Mona", Daddy's still alive. I'm going over to him. I think the Indians are gone now!"

"Posey don't leave me. I'll come too. Can be quiet."

Poinsettia climbed over the log, leaned down and extended her hand to Monique. "Take my hand, Mona, and come on. Hurry now."

The two sisters ran to their fallen father.

"Posey, his hair's missing. Why did they take Daddy's hair. Wipe his face off, Posey, he's all bloody."

The older daughter used her skirt's hem to wipe her dad's face. He opened his eyes and stared at his children. "Julie?" He moaned. "Julie? What of your Ma, Posey?"

"The Indians killed her, Daddy. Killed her before you got here. Mona and I were behind a big log. We hid when I saw Mama killed. She fell out of the wagon and an Indian jumped on her with his knife. Mona didn't see it happen, Daddy, only me!"

Feebly, John lifted a hand up and touched his daughter's face. "I'm dying, child. Be brave, now. Take your little sister and head back the way that we traveled this morning. Keep going until you reach the settlement. Stay alive! I love you!" His hand dropped to the ground and his eyes closed for the last time.

Posey folded her Dad's arms on his chest. "Mona, let's check on Ma. Be quick." The two children ran over to their mother's body. Julie's eyes stared vacantly at the sky. Posey arranged her mother's arms as she had her father's. "Ma's gone too. It is just us girls now, Mona. Come on, Dad said go. Come on." Posey took her sister's hand in hers and together they left the forest glade following the wagon track back the way they came.

The forest canopy withheld the sunlight, creating a forbidding appearance. Rustlings could be heard in the dried leaves that covered the forest floor. The two girls looked over their shoulders often as they moved along the trail. Poinsettia increased her pace slightly. "I'm the oldest. Come on, I'll go first, and you can follow me. "

"Posey, what happened to Daddy's head. Why was his hair gone. Why, Posey?"

"Indians took his hair, Mona."

Mona was quiet for a moment. "Did Daddy give them his hair, Posey, did he?"

"No, Mona, I don't think so. They just took it! Now, hush and don't make much noise, okay!"

The two girls walked on. The trail crossed a small brook. After wading across the brook, Posey turned and knelt on the last rock nearer the edge of the creek, cupped some water into her hands, and drank. The water was cool and fresh. "Here, Mona, come and get a drink before we go on. And wipe your face."

Their thirst quenched; the children walked along the trail.

"Posey, I'm getting hungry. Are you? Can we find something to eat. I didn't eat much breakfast before Ma put us in the wagon. And now I'm hungry."

Poinsettia sighed. "Maybe we can find some food soon. Shush! Can't you walk faster!" She tugged on her sister's hand, pulling her along. Farther down the trail a cluster of yellow and orange mushrooms, stacked like a pile of pancakes, were growing on the rough barked trunk of a large oak tree.

"Look!" Poinsettia exclaimed. She pointed at the bright cluster of mushrooms on the tree standing not far away from the trail's edge.

"Mona, remember when Mama took us to gather wild edibles from the forest to use in her spring stews. Look, doesn't that look like what Ma called Chicken, Chicken of the Woods?" Posey hurried over to the bed of mushrooms that encircled the roots and lower trunk of the large oak tree. "I believe they are. Mama said that they were better cooked, but, remember, she said we could nibble on them and if we didn't eat a lot of them raw, t'would be okay. Come on, let's try some!" Together the sisters filled their skirt pockets with the bright curly mushrooms and returned to the trail. Chewing mushroom bites eased the hunger cramps. Mona became quieter for a spell.

As the morning advanced, the bright sunlight deceptively hid an advancing storm. By midday, the sky turned a leaden color. The dark gray clouds obscured the light that filtered through the trees, turning the forest into a gloomy darkened shadowy sinister surrounding. The warmth began to fade as a breeze moved through the trees. The wind picked up. A sudden crash of thunder echoed off the mountain top and rolled through the forest. Another thunderous roar sounded shortly after the first. A deep darkness began to envelop the forest floor. Trees along the rutted trail cast threatening shadows across the path of the children. Quiet now, fingers tucked into her mouth, Mona's eyes rounded as she began to whimper.

The freshening storm was driving animals before it as they sought shelter from the lightning and thunder. A rabbit scampered across the path in front of the girls. Poinsettia saw a deer dash through the brush running ahead of the wind. It was followed by another. A small raccoon kit suddenly appeared in the wagon road just yards in front of the surprised girls. Mona dodged around Posey and started toward the baby coon when Posey grabbed her hair and pulled Mona to a stop.

"Posey, that hurts. Leggo my hair. I just wanna see it." Mona tried to push Posey's hands from her hair. "Let me go!" The little raccoon sat down in the trail and began uttering a high-pitched chirping noise.

Suddenly, a soft growl sounded as a large female coon rushed from beneath the trailside laurel and stood over her kit, snapping her jaws protectively at the two girls. Mona screamed. Posey froze. The female made a huffing, hissing sound and feinted toward the children. She sniffed loudly, and then uttering a grunt, satisfied that the two small humans posed no threat, she pushed the kit from the open trail into the bordering brush. She paused, turned her head toward Mona and Rose, hissed again, and led the small raccoon deeper into the surrounding undergrowth of the forest.

Posey adopted the voice that she had heard her mother Julia use when scolding. "You see. She could have eaten you and me for lunch, Mona. This is a wilderness. Think, girl, or we could get hurt. Best you stay behind me and let me make the decisions from now on. Not every animal that you see is gonna be friendly nor cuddly like that baby raccoon. You understand now?"

Eyes toward the ground, Mona nodded her head. Wind rustled the trees overhead. Light no longer filtered through the treetops. It was darker now than moments ago when the coons appeared. Scattered raindrops began to patter on the leaves overhead.

"C'mon, Mona, we need something to get under or we'll be wet and cold." Posey tugged her sister's arm. Stumbling along, Posey looked anxiously about for something that they could shelter under. A large fallen hickory tree lay across the trail, head-high to Posey. Forked near the top of the tree, the trunk was shrouded by two large sprawling leafy branches that hid the trail on the western and eastern side of the fallen trunk. Quick as the flash of lightning that illuminated the surrounding darkness, Posey pulled Mona under the tree trunk and sat down in the large space between the leafy branches. She felt secure. Feeling in her skirt pocket, she discovered a large piece of one of the mushrooms that they had harvested earlier that day. She broke the mushroom in half and shared it with her sister. After taking a bite, she breathed deep and stretched out on the ground. Mona lay back against her sister. A sudden crash of thunder shook the ground and the sheltering tree. Posey cried out, almost allowing her fear to surface. She felt Mona move closer against her. The thunder boomed again. Both girls whimpered. It was going to be a long sleepless night.

Daylight came. Posey stretched and yawned. Her dress was damp from the ground. Mona had fallen asleep after the storm. Posey slipped from her sister's embrace. She moved some of the leaves aside making a small opening that she could see through. Nothing large was moving. She crept from beneath the sheltering popular branches and stood erect. A bluejay darted overhead and perched on a tree branch. Posey was thirsty. Her mouth felt like dirt. She saw a small trickle of water on the hillside just past their makeshift shelter. It dribbled down the wooded slope and dripped from a rock shelf that overhung the wilderness road. She walked to the overhang and cupped her hands, catching the cool liquid. It tasted good, wet, clean, and cool. She caught handful after handful, slaking her thirst.

Satisfied, she brushed back a wisp of her brown hair, looked back over her shoulder, and called softly to Monique.

"Mona, come get some water. It's cool and fresh."

After struggling out from under the log, Mona joined her sister at the dripping rock's edge.

"Splash some in your face, Mona, and then use your hands, get a drink. You will feel better. Come on, get a drink, and we'll begin our day's walk. I don't know how far the settlement is, but we'll get there!"

Posey wandered to the far side of the trail from the spring. The tree line thinned, exposing a vast view across the hidden valley. A hundred feet or so below, another trail led upward toward the path that Posey and Mona traveled.

There was a rider coming up that trail. It was an Indian. His face was painted black and speckled with white dots. Black handprints adorned the white horse that he rode. Poinsettia gasped and covered her mouth with her hands, took one more look, and ran back to Mona. Tugging her arm, she led her sister back down the trail a yard or so to where a game trail entered the roadway from the hillside.

"Mona, we must hurry. There is an Indian coming up the hill, this way from the valley! On a big white horse."

Scurrying, slipping, sliding, the girls climbed the gravely game trail until it leveled out. They found themselves among small rocks and boulders atop the rock ledge that fed the dripping water. They paused to catch their breath.

"Let's gather some rocks, Mona. We can throw them at him or his horse if he sees us." Posey led the way to the base of the flat ledge. She placed some stones in her pocket. Mona did the same. Posey saw a large flat rock and struggled to pick it up. She carried it over to the edge of the overhang.

"Lie flat, Posey, lie flat!" Mona whispered hurriedly. "He'll have to look up to see us. Maybe we can drop a rock on him! You've got the biggest one. Do you think you can drop it and not fall off the ledge? You're the oldest, you know. I'll throw my rocks too." Mona whispered anxiously as her sister inched closer to the edge of the ledge, pushing the large flat rock nearer to the overhang's lip.

The sisters scooted to the edge of the rocky escarpment and peeked over. The Indian sat still on his horse, listening, checking his surroundings. But he never looked up before he dismounted. The warrior slid from the back of his horse and held the reins in his right hand and extended his left hand toward the dripping water. He saw the small footprints in the mud bordering the spring. He paused in motion. That's when Mona threw the first rock. It hit the horse. The horse jerked backward.

The Indian gripped the reins harder and pulled the horse toward him. In almost the same motion he looked up at Poinsettia as she dropped the large flat rock. It landed with a thud on the Indian's forehead just as he looked upward toward the ledge. His knees buckled and he collapsed into the roadway.

Posey and Mona jumped up simultaneously. "We did it. We hit him. Let's go see if he has any food."

Mona scrambled across the rocky ledge back to the game trail and started down with Posey right behind. Reaching the bottom of the hill, the two girls ran to the fallen brave. Posey's rock had done its job. The Indian wasn't moving. Posey saw his knife scabbard and jerked the long-bladed knife from it. His tomahawk lay by his side and his right hand still grasped the horse's reins. Posey tried to pull the reins from the Indian's clutched fingers, but his locked grasp was too tight. "I'm tired of walking now!" She put the knife down and grabbed the tomahawk and to Mona's horror, Posey slashed its blade down toward the grasping fingers that held the reins. A flash of bright metal, a slow flow of red, and the fingers fell limp from the Indian's right hand, releasing the horse's reins. Quick as a flash, Posey had the reins and pulled the horse away from the fallen man.

Mona found a pouch filled with some type of greasy mixture that looked as if it might be food. She tasted it and wrinkled her nose. But it was food. She placed a pinch of it in her mouth and chewed slowly. It was greasy, but there were dry berries and meat in the mixture. She took it over to Posey and showed it to her. "Here, Posey, it's not too terribly bad. It's some kind of food. Eat some."

"Later, Mona. We've walked far enough. Let's find out if his horse will let us ride it. The girls led the horse along the trail until they found a stump that they could stand on to mount the horse. The animal didn't fear the children and stood still while Mona got on his back. Then Posey grasped the reins in her left hand and mounted behind her sister. She drew the reins to the right, turning the animal up the trail, nudged his ribs with her heels lightly, and grinned as the horse trotted along the forest path.

Later in the afternoon they rode into a meadow where the family had spent a night some days before. Posey recognized the meadow. A rock fire pit that their father had arranged lay near the bank of the stream. Reining in the horse, they dismounted and watered the animal and then tied him to a long spruce branch that hung low to the ground. After pulling the Indian's blanket from the horse's back, the two girls spread it on the ground, lay down and chewed the last of the Indian's dry greasy food. They pulled the blanket over themselves and drifted off to sleep as the sun set.

Daylight saw Alex, Billy, and Tobias the Indian ride into the meadow. They halted their horses at the eastern edge of the grassy field and stared at the white horse with the black painted hands that stood tethered to a spruce tree. The horse's left forefoot's stocking was black.

"Odd." Tobias thought. "Only one Injun marks his horses with the black hand mark. I know of that Injun. He bad news Injun"

Just past the horse was an Indian blanket covering a small lump. The lump wiggled and a young girl sat up, rubbed her eyes, looked over the grass at the three riders, saw them, and ducked back under the blanket!

The three riders eased their mounts over to the Indian blanket. Billy dismounted beside the wiggling blanket. He pulled the edge of the covering back exposing a very sleepy small girl and a larger one who jumped to her feet scowling fiercely and waving a tomahawk. Glaring at them, she demanded an immediate answer. "Just who are you and let go my blanket!"

Alex dismounted. Tobias took their mounts and pack horses and rode over to the Indian pony. He dismounted and strung a rope between two trees and tethered their five horses plus the Indian mount to the rope, allowing them to graze on the long blue green grass. He eyed the paint markings on the strange mare, then rejoined the group at the old campsite. Billy had gathered wood and started a blaze and was occupied in preparations for a morning meal.

Alex stood between Billy and the two girls. He had asked who they were and calmed their fears somewhat. "I bet you are hungry. Are you?" Mona nodded her head. "Yes, I am. And my sister, her name's Posey, and she's hungry too." Alex smiled. Well, Billy over there's gonna fix some breakfast. You can eat with us." He turned toward his cousin and Tobias and made the introductions. "This wee lassie is Monique, Mona Vaughn. And this young lady is her big sister Poinsettia Posey Vaughn. They are the sole survivors of an Indian attack on their family's wagon. It appears to have happened about three days past farther ahead on the wagon trail west."

Posey interrupted. "We fled after our parents were killed and have had little to subsist on other than water, some mushrooms, and some Indian's dried food. It was greasy but it had meat and some berries mixed with it. But we ate it all yesterday."

Tobias grunted. "Probably pemmican of some sort."

Alex pointed at the bearded man hovering over the fire. "So, girls, Billy's fixing to fry up some sow belly bacon and corn dodgers along with some coffee. Suit you to eat some of that?"

Tobias pointed at the tethered horses. "How you come by Storm Cloud's white mare with the black stocking? Him bad Injun, Chickasaw warrior. Raise many soba', horses. He marks all his horses with black hand. How you get horse?"

Mona spoke out loudly. "My sister dropped a big rock on that Indian's head, and she whacked his fingers off to get the horse's reins. I threw rocks at the horse."

The three men chuckled. Billy grinned. "Wee lassies, these two, but tough."

"Seems that they have no living relatives. At least none known to the girls. I've told them they could go with us if you agree. So what say you, Billy and Tobias?" Alex asked.

Billy looked up from the cook fire. "Doesn't seem as how we can leave them here in the wilderness. Might as well take them on. Looks like they have their own mount."

Alex nodded. "Next settlement or post we reach; we probably need to get them some possibles. They look a bit threadbare."

Tobias grunted. "Small girls, won't eat much." He sat down by the fire.

Alex smiled at the girls. "Looks like you've joined up with us.

You can consider us your kin now. So, there's some hot food. Go get something to eat and then we'll head on west afterward.

A couple of days later the party rode into the scene of the Vaughn family's tragedy. The three men buried the remains of the dead parents. Alex found John Vaughns still saddled horse grazing just beyond the abandoned wagon. The two draft horses were gone, the traces having been cut. Evidently, the saddled horse had broken loose from the Indians and wandered back along the trail.

Alex checked the animal out thoroughly. The horse had no wounds and its feet were sound. It seemed gentle enough. He led the horse over to the waiting group and asked Posey, "Can your sister ride alone. Is she able to handle her own mount?"

"She is. Daddy taught her two years ago. She's not afraid of the horses." Posey answered Alex.

"You're talking about me. Yes, I know how to ride. Posey's right. My daddy taught me. That's his big horse that you found. It knows me. I have ridden it alone before." Mona stated firmly.

Alex grinned. "Okay, young'un. Drop down that Injun's horse and climb up on your dad's horse. But if I see that you can't handle him, you'll have to share with your sister. Okay?"

Quick as a flash, Mona slid from behind her sister off of the white horse and ran toward her Dad's animal. She climbed up onto the saddle and Alex handed her the reins. The party, all well mounted now, moved down the trail again.

CHAPTER SIX

Monique Mona Vaughn

Alex and his party halted on the bank of the Coosa River near a rock-strewn shallow ford. In the distance a mountain peak filled the horizon above the forest's tree line. After refreshing their mounts and filling their canteens from the clear water of the river, they forded the river at this narrow point and took a trail that climbed north toward the mountain peak. They made camp at nightfall in a forest glade. The elevation had changed just enough so that the air felt crisper, dryer, and cooler.

The next morning the travelers began a gradual ascent along the mountain trail bound for the large Creek Indian trading post on the Coosa River. A week had passed since Posey's and Mona's rescue. The children had relaxed and accepted the three men as their protectors.

A morning haze filtered through the trees bordering the trail. Midway up the mountain side, the party's path led them across a small creek and up the side of the mountain slope covered in loose shale. Alex led the procession, followed by Tobias, then the girls now on separate mounts, and with Billy bringing up the rear. The narrow trail was bare of tree and brush cover. Alex's mount had just topped the rise and entered the bordering forest when he heard a scream. He twisted in his saddle just in time to see Mona's horse rear up, nostrils flaring, forelegs flailing the air, and fling itself backward off the incline. Mona, the young rider, still mounted, was carried by the falling horse toward the creek seventy-five feet below. She screamed again as she and her horse fell through the air. Mona and her horse landed in a shallow pool with the girl pinned beneath the horse's back. Billy turned his mount on the narrow trail and quickly descended to the creek bottom. He dismounted and ran splashing to the side of the fallen horse. The animal was struggling to rise. Billy grabbed the bridle and held the Bay in place as it struggled to its feet, attempting to prevent the young rider from being dragged by the rising horse.

Mona's body fell from the saddle as the horse rose from the water. She never stirred. The saddle horn had pierced her chest. There was very little blood. The swift moving creek water had washed it away.

Posey joined Billy in the creek, grabbing her younger sister's arm. "Mona, Mona, oh, Mona. Don't leave me now, sister. You are all that's left in my family. Mona, Ma's gone and so is Papa. Mona, please, Mona, not you too!" Tears of anguish streamed down Poinsettia's face as Billy tenderly lifted the small body from the water and waded to the creek's bank. There, he laid Mona on a bed of moss and grass.

Alex and Tobias dismounted. Tobias retrieved Mona's horse. Alex looked at the shattered and distraught Posey. Then, tenderly, he put his arm around the young girl.

"Poinsettia, we'll take her with us and get off this mountain. You'll be with us. So will Mona. You'll be alright."

Alex glanced toward Billy. "Take a blanket and wrap Mona in it. Let's get mounted and complete the climb to the valley beyond. Then we'll decide what we'll do."

The group remounted. Alex looked at Posey and said, "Hold on to your saddle horn. I'll lead your horse up the incline. Don't look down."

The afternoon that followed Mona's accidental death had been very somber. The four survivors had not spoken much. Along about dark, they had made camp on the far side of the mountain. Posey, exhausted after grieving for her sister all afternoon, had finally fallen asleep.

Alex lay in thought for some time staring at the sky overhead that was brilliantly lit with stars. "Tomorrow, in the morning, we need to find a memorable spot to bury Mona. And, then I guess it's about time to settle down. We've come a far piece in the year or so since that mess at Fort Hawkins. Now I guess it's time for me and Billy to choose a place for a homestead. Looks like we've adopted a girl child to raise. We three, Billy and I along with Tobias are all she has left now." He fell asleep.

When Alex awoke in the morning, Tobias had a cook fire going. Billy had the coffee brewing and was cooking the last of their venison in a skillet while a plate of biscuits warmed near the fire.

Alex threw off his blankets, picked up his saddle, and headed for the picket line and their horses. While breakfast was still cooking, Tobias and Alex saddled the four mounts and placed the lightened loads on the pack horses.

Posey awoke and joined them at the fire. Billy spoke first.

"Let's head on down off of this mountain and move on west." Tobias nodded in agreement and looked at Alex who said,

"Sounds good to me. I've been thinking that it is about time to look for a piece of land that is suitable for a homestead and where we could build a trading post. Billy, you and I have spoken of this supposed partnership for a spell, off and on. I think we're probably far enough into the territory now so that we can pick and choose a site without asking any government's permission. Poinsettia, do you think you'd like to consider us three men your family until your grown? We would take good care of you. And, Billy's cooking is improving. What would you think of that, a new homestead and three grown brothers?

Posey bowed her head for a moment, looked up at the three men who watched her intently, and grinned. "I think that would be just fine. I'd like that a lot."

Alex sighed. "Well now, that's all settled. Billy, you and Tobias agree?" Billy chuckled and Tobias's lips moved toward an almost smile.

"Looks as if you've got three brothers, Posey. Finish your breakfast and let's head on down this mountain."

As the riders neared the edge of the plateau and rode out of the forest, they were able to catch a glimpse of what lay beyond the mountain. In the distance, they could see a green valley with a silvery creek running through it. The trail from the bluff led toward the valley. Alex turned his horse onto the trail and led his band of travelers toward a new horizon. An hour later, the trail leveled out and they rode into a pleasant valley. Alex halted his horse near a stand of tall birch trees. A grassy meadow stretched 200 yards toward the creek that they had seen from the bluff.

Posey's horse stood near Alex's mount. Posey looked up at Alex. "Mona would like it here. Don't you think so?"

Alex pointed at a small hill on the south side of the meadow. "There, over there. That hill seems a likely resting place. I suspect that Mona would be comfortable there. And here, where we stand, we can erect a house. And over yonder to the west, a building for a store, with a barn just to the side."

"Sounds mighty fine to me. I'm gonna miss Mona. At least she'll be here, near me, for a while. Thank you, Alex." A tear trickled down Posey's face. It was settled.

CHAPTER SEVEN

Herman The German

Alex finished saddling his horse and leaned against the animal and looked across the saddle at the nearby cabin and the larger trading post building.

"Just as I reckoned," he thought. "That stand of nearby popular trees provided straight logs of a uniform length for the cabin. We cut two window openings for interior lighting and a door that fronted the building. Cutting the planks to fashion the window and door coverings was the hardest part, I guess.

Billy suggested that we rafter the roof and overlay it with small logs; and then as time permitted, make shingles or use sawn planking to cover those for waterproofing."

Alex hung his saddlebags on the small iron knob behind the saddle and then shoved his long rifle into the sheath beneath the saddle's cinch strap.

"Took forever or so it seemed to get the rocks from the creek bank to build the fireplace. I wonder how long that grassed clay filler will hold as a binder for the stacked stones. We finished the cabin by the end of May and were well along on the barn's construction. And now here it is the first week of September, the corral and the barn are built and so is the store building. The only thing left to complete is cutting enough flat planking to cover the dirt floors in the cabin and trading post's building."

He walked over to the barn where Billy was saddling his mare. "You still comfortable with our partnership plans?" Alex inquired.

"Billy nodded yes. "Why not. We're kin, we've come this far together since 1812..and, its just business, being a Scot, I like to make money, don't you! See any other trading posts in the valley. Looks like we just might be gonna enjoy a monopoly. And, just as we learned when we counted our pokes the other night that we have enough money to begin stocking the place with merchandise and have some more left over for the unexpected, just in case. Right?"

"Yep." Alex grinned. "It's two days or more on horseback to that old Alexander McGillivray trading post located at Apple Grove Plantation on the lower Coosa River. Guess we ought to get started. Reckon Tobias and Miss Poinsettia are ready?

"Me ready. Born ready! You two speak loud. I heard." Tobias called from the barn door. "Posey, she took her horse and walked down to her sister Mona's grave, say goodbye for a spell."

"Well, let's get on with it then." Alex placed his foot in the stirrup and lifted himself into the saddle, turned his mount about, clicked his tongue, and cantered the short distance across the homestead yard to Posey. She saw him coming and mounted her horse. All four riders turned and headed south following the creek down the valley.

They followed the creek gradually moving southeast toward the larger Coosa river and the trading site. The second day dawned with not a cloud in the sky. Along about noon, they rested the horses on a grassy knoll above a bend of the Coosa River. In the distance, they could see wisps of smoke from the chimneys of the village.

Billy grunted, "Looks like the place is humming. Lot of chimneys spewing smoke. More than one or two!"

"You hear all of that racket down in the holler?" Alex looked over at Billy.

Tobias cantered up. He had ridden ahead scouting the trail. "Lot of noise back down there." He jerked his head backwards.

Posey's girl voice joined in. "Well, let's go see what all the fuss is about. Or are you men just going to sit here astride your horses and talk about it all the livelong day."

Alex grinned. "She ain't never at a loss for words, is she. C'mon, let's go see what's ahead."

The party of four riders heard loud hammering and trees falling mingled with coarse yells as they neared their destination. Rounding a bend in the road, they saw the source of the noise. Many workmen, white and black, were removing brush from the area fronting them, creating a huge clearing. Trees were being felled by one band of men. Another group was cutting the downed timber into smaller sections for firewood. Lanes had been cleared through the forest, brush piles were being burned, rows of rough-hewn log benches had been erected for seating, and all of that expended effort had created a manmade clearing . The rows of log benches faced a small stage erected at the head of the newly cleared space.

"What in dickens are they building?" Billy wondered out loud. "They're clearing enough room for an army!"

A voice roared from behind the riders. "An army of the Lord's, Sir. That's what's coming!" Alex and Billy swung their horses about and faced the voice. A large full bodied heavy-set man with a full growth of face whiskers parted the brush and stepped into the clearing in front of the four travelers.

"An army of the Lord, no less than hundreds, nay, thousands, I suspect! Or I'm not the Most Reverend Phineas T. Spurgeon, at your service!" Spurgeon ducked his head forward in an exaggerated bow toward the four riders. "Indeed, we're preparing for the largest tent revival ever to hit the 'Bama' backwoods. And we're bringing repentance and the gospel not just to our white brethren settlers, but to those enslaved Africans and the red barbarians of the Indian Nations. Where you folks coming from?"

Billy spoke first. "We're opening a trading post on the creek this side of that mountain with the tall trees that look like a flag atop it. Somewhat north of here."

"Sounds like you're talking about what we've called Commons Creek hereabouts. Well, you're coming down for this camp meeting, are you." Spurgeon asked.

Alex squinted at the man. "Hadn't heard about it. Thought that we'd purchase some supplies and maybe a new dress for our young lady here. Is there still a source of supplies here."

"Certainly is, sir. Goodfellows and Knight Company, they have an excellent supply warehouse in the heart of our settlement, what the folks that came with General Scott call Alabama Town."

Tobias leaned over to Poinsettia. "We gonna fix you up real pretty, young lady. We've all agreed. You need a new bonnet, some slippers besides them moccasins I made you, and a couple of dresses. Something softer and frillier than buckskin breeches."

Posey grinned at Tobias. "Maybe a couple of ribbons, too. I like red and blue ones. And, just maybe, a piece of candy or a gum drop or two." Posey smiled in her girlish shy way and shook her horse's reins, trotting away.

Tobias grinned and spurred his horse into a trot. The four riders rapidly advanced down the roadway and into the busy community of Alabama Town.

Alex slowed his mount to a walk. "We need a livery first. See if we can acquire a couple or three pack horses at a good price. There!" He pointed to a board fronted building surrounded by a corral. A sign nailed to the corral fence read 'Walt's Stable-Hay, Horses, and cattle, pigs too'.

"Billy, why don't you take Posey and see if you can find us lodgings for tonight and tomorrow night. We'll need two rooms, one for us men and another for Poinsettia. Tobias and I will dicker for some horses."

"Okay, but remember something, Alex. I like eggs and we haven't really had any since we left Carolina almost 5 years ago now. Maybe, if that livery sells livestock, they might have a couple of chickens that we could carry back with us, and a rooster. Or maybe know someone who does. Okay?"

"I won't forget your egg hunger. See what I can do." Alex dismounted and wrapped his horse's reins around one of the corral posts. Tobias did the same and the two men moved toward the livery barn in search of the proprietor.

"Posey, looks like its up to us two to locate lodgings and a few baths for the four of us would be good." He sniffed his underarm and wrinkled his nose. "Watcha think, girl?"

Posey grinned. "Spect that its time, Billy. C'mon, let's get it done."

They rode down the road toward the river. A long fronted two-story frame building stood on the left roadside. It was fronted by a low covered porch lined with chairs and a bench or two. A small sign that read 'Ma's Beds and Meals' overhung the stairs leading up to the porch. The pair dismounted and with Posey in the lead entered the building's large front room.

A buxom matronly woman dusting a shelf behind the hotel's counter turned to face Poinsettia and Billy as they entered.

"Afternoon, folks." She spoke first. "My, what a beautiful young traveler. Y'all seeking lodging for the night?"

Billy doffed his hat and nodded in the affirmative. "Yes'm. We are. There will be four of us. I'd like a separate room for the wee lassie here, and another room for the three of us men. And a bathing tub and water for her." He nodded toward Poinsettia. "Is there a bath house where us men can go?"

"My name's Madelyn, Madelyn Prentiss." The woman spoke softly. "Most folks here abouts call me Ma Prentiss. I can fix you up. Take the first two rooms at the top of the stairs on the right. The first room has two beds, ought to serve you and your other menfolk just right. Give the next room to this young lady. I'll see that there's a bath that is prepared for her shortly. There's a tub in that room. Meanwhile, you men can go just next door to Joe, he's the barber. He has a small bathhouse set up behind his shop. Cost you a quarter each with hot water and towels. And two bits for a shave, another two bits for a hair cut. If'n the other two men are as shaggy as you, y'all could use his services.
 How long you want the rooms?"

"Two nights. We should be leaving by Friday morning late." Billy pulled his poke from under his shirt. "How much?"

"A dollar a night each for four people. Add the girl's bath. Em, let's see. Make it, say, Four dollars and a quarter. That'll be eight dollars and a half for the time you mentioned."

Billy handed over the necessary coins.

Ma Prentiss bit one of the silver coins. "Don't get a lot of hard coins around here. Pleasure to see these. Where you folks coming from?"

"We hail from Carolina, South Carolina, mostly. Plan to start a trading post up near the mountain back yonder a ways. Where you folks know the area as Commons Creek." Billy said.

"Well then, welcome. Here's your keys and enjoy your stay."

Posey and Billy turned toward the door. "Lil Sister, let's put our gear in the rooms and then go find that Goodfellows store that the preacher was speaking about, what say you. Get you some new duds before you get all cleaned up."

Posey impetuously hugged Billy's neck. "Thank you. I'd really like that a lot."

Goodfellows and Knight Emporium read the bright red and white sign that hung over the door of the large log building across the dirt street from the local tavern. A wagon stood outside the building. Tobias stepped from between the wagon and the building's porch just as Posey and Billy rode over from the boarding house.

"What's with the wagon, Tobias?"

"Alex, he buy it. Livery only had one pack horse for sale. So bought wagon instead. Did have three chickens, rooster too. They're in the wagon in a coop. Figured you'd ask. See!" and Tobias lifted the canvas flap for Billy and Poinsettia so they could view the chickens.

They entered the Emporium together. The men left Poinsettia to her own devices while they looked over the store's inventory and compiled a list of items for their new enterprise. Posey saw the dry goods tables in the rooms center and began making her selections.

"Wish Mona could have been here. She would have enjoyed choosing her dress, probably would have wanted it in her favorite color of blue." Posey's eyes misted.

A young female clerk crossed the room to Posey's side. "Good day, ma'am. I'm Sue Ellen. Can I help you with an item?"

"I could use help, yes indeed. A new dress with a nice petticoat, suitable for everyday wear; and another one, maybe, if there was a reason to be a little fancy. And a pair of shoes and a bonnet. And I want some hair ribbons. I really like red ribbons. And a new comb. And some candy."

The clerk smiled. "That's quite a list. Let's see what I can do."

An hour or so later, Billy and Poinsettia returned to the boarding house laden with Posey's wrapped purchases.

"Posey, here's your room key. Take your new gear and go enjoy yourself. Ma said that she would have you a bath prepared when you returned. I'll let her know you are back. And lock the door. You're in a settlement now and other people are about. So, take some precautions."

Posey nodded, handed her horse's reins over to Billy, filled her arms with packages, and climbed the stairs onto the porch.

Billy rode over to the livery stable and boarded their two mounts then made his way back to the room reserved for Alex, Tobias, and himself.

It wasn't long before Tobias and Alex knocked on the door and called out, awakening Billy from napping. The men entered and hung their slickers and saddle bags on the wall mounted clothes rack.

"Well, that's done. Tomorrow the men at the Emporium will have our orders ready. They'll load the wagon for us there at the Emporium and we can start back to the homestead on Friday morning." Alex stated. "Supplies and all cost a bit more than I expected, what with the wagon and the team, oh, and the chickens. We had planned on about $ 70.00 or so. Ended up being nearer $ 200.00. But we needed a wagon."

"What all did you purchase for our wintering and to stock the trading post?" Billy asked.

"Well, first off, since we haven't put in a crop yet, we'll need hay for the stock during the winter. I ordered some and it will be hauled up to us next month. Then, I looked after our staples needed for our winter's existence. Sugar, flour, some potatoes, a couple of cured hams, salt, two sacks of coffee beans along with one of them new-fangled coffee grinders and some soap bars. Speaking of which, is there gonna be a place here where we can bathe?"

"There is. And you two need it for sure. It's next door at Barber Joe's. You've got a few hours yet. What else did you order?"

"Billy, for the trading post, I had them add four casks of corn likker, good Kentucky brewed stuff. A barrel of salt, some pants and shirts, another 50 pounds of coffee beans, 40 pounds of lead ingots for bullets, 6 kegs of gunpowder, a box of rifle flints, a couple of dozen trading knives, a small keg of whale oil for the guns and lamps along with candles and matches. We can begin trading with all of that, then come back for more if we need it before spring. Oh, and I added a half dozen muskets to the list and three more pistols. They always trade well to our redskin brethren or new settlers passing by."

Tobias grunted. "Me in need of a bath, you both too. Let's go find this Joe man. Is Posey alright?"

Billy laughed. "She has her new outfits and is enjoying a bath in her room. You both can gawk and exclaim on how great she looks later! And I bet she will, she's always been a pretty lass anyway and with them fancy duds, I suspect that she'll turn a head or two. Let's go to Joe's, and then afterward, maybe find some vittles. My belly is beginning to think that some Injun's cut my throat. No offense meant to you, Tobias!"

Daylight found Alex leading their string of horses to the livery's blacksmith for shoeing. He returned to the boarding house and met the others in the dining room for breakfast. Poinsettia was seated near the head of the table resplendent in a new dress with her shoulder length hair styled in a sleek low chignon. The bun at the nape of her neck was secured with a new scarlet ribbon.

Alex was in awe. The young girl's beauty was breathtaking.

Louder than normal, a background sound similar to a low rumbling was heard as the group at the table was finishing their meal. Billy and Alex turned and looked toward the door.

"That almost sounds like low thunder!" Alex muttered.

"Has more of a human sound, like singing in a monotone. Listen!" Billy pushed his chair back from the table and walked to the window. The chanting sounds were drawing closer. Faint words could be recognized, some sounding like 'At the cross, at the cross, where I first saw the light...' and then 'Come, ye thankful people, come, raise the song of harvest home; all is safely gathered in, ere the winter storms begin...'

Ma Prentiss spoke up from the doorway to the kitchen. "Sounds as if all of the newcomers and visitors are headed over to the new grove for the camp meeting's first service. Ought to be a busy day today. Rest of the week should be entertaining as well. I even heard that the Sheriff was gonna release the few prisoners in the town's jail so they could attend. Said it might could do them some good!"

"What happens at a camp meeting?" Posey inquired.

Ma smiled indulgently at the teenager. "Why, child, round abouts here in the territories, folks can't attend a regular church service. So, there's always people that have never met their Lord Jesus or confessed their sins and short-comings. Gives them an introduction to salvation. Many couples are waiting on ministers that can marry them up so's they're not living in a state of sin and now can be socially acceptable. And then there's children that need to learn the gospel and folks to baptize; that's the reason for clearing that grove of trees near the creek. The parsons can baptize their new converts in the creek. Big doings here abouts for at least a week or two."

Poinsettia looked questioningly at Billy, Tobias, and Alex. "Could we go see what this camp meeting's all about? I'd really like to attend. Something out of the ordinary, you know."

Tobias grunted. "I am curious too. White men do strange things. Different from Indian way."

Billy grinned. "You ought to fit right in, Tobias. Nothing at all different about you. No war dancing though. But you can chant some. Probably fit in real good since you think you can sing!"

"You guys quit jawing at each other. Posey and I know that you mean no harm and are funning about, others might not. But yeah, it would be different. C'mon. Let's walk off that good breakfast and go see what's doing. Ma, you want to come along with us?"

Ma Prentiss removed her apron and hung it on the back of one of the table chairs. "Why not, Mr. Avery. I could stand some religion. Been a spell since I've heard anyone preaching from the 'Good Book', the Bible, especially out here."

With that in mind, Alex Avery's group and Ma Prentiss walked out onto the boarding house porch. Ma pulled the door closed as she exited the building. They joined the throng of townspeople heading toward the newly timbered grove at the end of town.

As the party neared the clearing, a male voice, loud, resonant, and sonorous rang through the air. At a distance, on an elevated platform, a heavy-set man, dressed in black, with a mane of thick black hair, was speaking through a short silver colored speaking trumpet.

"Why, we met him yesterday as we were coming into town. That's the Reverend. Reverend Phineas T. Spurgeon is what he called himself!" Billy exclaimed. "It surely is. Listen, just listen to him."

Reverend Spurgeon's voice boomed through the air's distance from the podium.

" And God's son said or so we're told in the New Testament book of Matthew, chapter 11, beginning with verse 28, 'Come unto me all ye that labour, and are heavy laden, and I will give you rest.' And that's just the beginning of our Lord's promise, Pilgrims. Have you heard this call? Are you coming to the Lord. Listen, children, to what else He has to say."

The minister breathed deep and bellowed through the speaking trumpet. "Jesus said next 'Take my yoke upon you and learn of me; for I am meek and lowly in heart, and you shall find rest for your souls.' Have you learned of Jesus, God's Son. Have you taken him into your heart? Can you feel the power?"

Huge numbers of people in the crowd before the podium's stage began swaying left to right, in cadence with the speaker's deep and resonant voice. It almost hypnotized the crowd. Then one large full-figured woman uttered a shrill yes, almost a scream, and tumbled to the ground. The crowd took up the chant, "Yes, come to the Lord, yes, yes! And the swaying increased. Soon the fallen woman was joined by others dropping to the ground. Some knelt and called in prayer, others wailed, some were shrieking.

Poinsettia turned to Alex. "That minister, he's telling these people about the same Jesus, God's Son, that my dead Ma and Pa taught my sister Mona and me about? Am I correct?"

"Yes, you are, Posey. All of us that believe in God know the story of God's Son. And we know just as you learned at your mama's lap, that if you believe in Jesus, then you are saved. This is what so many of these people are hearing for the first time."

"Alex, I think that I would like to learn more about Jesus. Can that man down there tell me?"

"Your folks taught you to read. I'll see if the Emporium has a Bible that they'll sell me. That way you can take it home with us and study it, probably learn more of what you're asking as you can read it any time that you have a question. And in the meantime, if you want to ask a question of the good Reverend Spurgeon, I feel sure that he'd welcome the question and probably render you a long answer. I'm glad that you asked, Posey, I should have bought a Bible for all of us to use a long time ago."

Ma Prentiss interrupted Alex and Posey. "Look! Lookie yonder. There's our sheriff bringing his three prisoners from the town jail. See that big tall feller. That's the one known hereabouts as Herman the German. He's bad to drink too much. Then he's been known to pick fights and bust things up. I won't let him eat at my boarding house because of his behavior."

The party walked back to town. The early afternoon was spent in making last minute purchases for the startup of their new trading post. The Emporium had some Bibles. Sue Ellen, the clerk, helped Posey pick one for herself and her new brothers.

"Our store received a crate of these fine Bibles just last week. We expected a demand for them by the attendees of the Camp Meeting. It's been well talked about. And now you are the first to purchase one. Well, almost the first, cause I bought one for me too." Sue Ellen smiled at Posey and handed her the Holy Book.

Their shopping completed, Alex returned to the livery stable and checked on the blacksmith's shoeing of their animals. All seemed in readiness. He had one last chore. With the new horses tethered, he notched each animal's right ear with a v notch and a slash for identification, just as he had their other stock back at the homestead. Then he poured some turpentine on the fresh cuts for healing purposes. Finished with the animals, Alex started back to the boarding house to rejoin his people. A noisy throng was gathered near the front porch steps of Ma Prentiss's.

A tall wide shouldered and heavily muscled man was shoving people off the steps and into the street. "I'm hungry," the man bellowed, "and Ma's got the best meals. I'm going to eat here!"

Ma Prentiss appeared with a broom in her hand attempting to bar the doorway. "Herman, I've told you afore now, you aren't welcome in my boarding house. You tear things up."

"Well, maybe this time I won't. I've given up the demon rum now. Yes I have. Sheriff said I had been jailed long enough, for me to get out of his space and try to behave. So, I'm hungry. I've got one dollar. I've had it since the night before I got thrown into the jailhouse and I want a meal with spuds and gravy!" And with that he shoved Ma Prentiss aside. She fell, then struggled to her feet and soundly whacked Herman the German over the head with her broom. The broomstick broke. Herman jerked one half of the broom from Ma's hands and shook it in her direction.

"You shouldn't have done that, you old bitty. I just want to eat, not be whacked with a broomstick. Maybe its you that needs a whacking!"

Alex jumped onto the porch, shoved through the throng of on-lookers, and jerked Herman the German around to face him. Then he slammed his right fist into Herman's nose and knocked him against the wall.

"Get inside, Ma, get inside!" Alex yelled. Herman stood up and gathered his senses just as Alex hit him again. This time, Herman lunged back against Alex. The two men crashed against a roof support, breaking it in half and tumbled into the street. The roof sagged and onlookers scambled out of the way. Herman jumped to his feet and slammed a foot against Alex's shoulder, pinning him down.

"A duel, I challenge you to a duel, stranger. Who are you anyway?" Herman bellowed.

One of the townsmen spoke loudly to the German. "That fellow you've just challenged is a newcomer, Herman." The man guffawed. "He might just get the best of you. We don't know him from Adam's housecat! Better let him up and back off, Herman."

"All that true, stranger. Are you a big bad dude. What you wanna fight me with?"

"Mister, I have no quarrel with you except for your pushing Ma Prentiss around. You apologize and there's no reason to fight. Just tell her you were wrong."

"I don't apologize. What do you want to fight me with. Answer now."

"I don't want to choose. You choose. You started this whole ruckus. You need to try to finish it...if you kin! Get your damn foot off my shoulder and let's do this!"

"Okay, I'll choose. You have a knife on your belt. I got one too. Let's use them and don't wait. Do it now, stranger! Do it now." Herman screamed his anger.

The scattergun's blast rent the air. Everyone stood hard and fast. "What's going on down here. Herman, I just released you from jail. What are you doing now, starting another fight? You gonna get yourself kilt one of these days, you crazy German!" The sheriff cocked the other barrel on his shotgun.

"Now, maybe, Stranger, you might want to pack up and leave town, let Herman here cool off by spending another night behind bars."

"Sheriff," Alex dusted himself off, "The big fellow started it by picking on Ma. He challenged me to a duel. I hail from South Carolina. We don't take lightly to ignoring challenges or an invite to a duel, so I guess if you'll be so kind as to look aside for a few minutes, I'll humor the overgrown lout."

Alex withdrew his long-bladed belt knife from its sheath and stepped into the street. "So, Herman the German, you wanted a fight and issued a challenge, jerk your blade and come on over here. Time's a'wasting!"

Herman roared, pulled a knife from his boot, and lunged into the street toward Alex. The German swung high. Alex side-stepped the swing and slammed his knife's hilt into Herman's forehead. The blow was hard, hard enough so that witnesses swore that they heard the bone crack. Herman's eyes rolled back into his head as he fell unconscious face down into the street.

Lightning couldn't have been faster. Alex straddled Herman's back, sat down on the man, leaned forward with his knife in his right hand and as his knife blade flashed in the afternoon sun, he deftly sliced a v-notch and a slash in Herman the German's right ear. He wiped his knife blade off on his pants leg and stood up. Herman was coming to. He groaned and rolled over, suddenly realizing that his ear had been cut. He wiped his hand across his ear and stared at the blood smeared in the palm of his hand. He struggled to get on his feet.

Alex held his hand out toward Herman. "You lost, big man. And now you'll wear my brand the rest of your life...or cut off your ear. Either way, you've been notched with a slash-V, my brand. I've given you your life. Now you owe me a life."

Herman looked at the extended hand. He grinned. "Guess you must be one bad dude." And he took the extended hand and stood up as Alex pulled him to his feet.

"I could use a man with your strength in our outfit. Want to start over and ride to my holdings and our new trading post on Commons Creek with me and my partners?"

"I could do that. But I gotta have something to eat first."

"Apologize to Ma. I'd bet she'll feed you then. You have a last name, Herman?"

"Schiller, Herman Schiller. And I will apologize. And go with you."

"Sounds good to me, Herman Schiller. Gather your gear and be ready. Meet you at the livery tomorrow morning. We leave at first light. Now go tell Ma that you're sorry...and get some of her good grub."

The sheriff shook his head, uncocked his scattergun, muttered to himself "I ain't never seen nothing like that!" and walked toward his office.

CHAPTER EIGHT

Storm Cloud

Daylight found the party of five mounted and enroute toward their homestead. The first night out they made camp near the halfway mark of their journey home. Following their meal the discussion around the campfire centered on work awaiting them on their arrival tomorrow or the next day at their homestead.

"Too many men now." Billy spoke first. "I think that Posey will need a bit more privacy now that Herman has joined us. There's only two rooms in that cabin and one of those has only a curtain partition for a wall. We need another cabin."

Alex nodded. "Aye, so we do. And we kin do it. I suggest that you and Posey get the supplies stored and then arrange the merchandise in our new trading post building. Meanwhile, Tobias, Herman, and I can cut the necessary logs and drag them over from the forest to begin the new cabin or bunk house. We should have it under roof with a chimney and fireplace within three weeks barring weather. Then all we will need to do is cut enough firewood to see us through a spell."

Tobias nodded and Herman grunted in agreement. That settled, the group turned in for the night.

The trail ride the next day was uneventful. They reached the homestead a couple of hours before dark. All seemed in order. After unloading the wagon, corralling the new stock, and while Herman erected a temporary chicken coop for the new flock, Alex rode around the homestead's perimeter. The back of his neck tingled a bit. Something just wasn't right. As he crossed their watering brook, he spotted a footprint in the soft bank. Alex dismounted and leading his horse, inspected the footprint. It was definitely that of a man. Probably tall by the look of the stride length between two prints. The track wasn't fresh, maybe three days old. But it had been made by a single person wearing moccasins; and judging by the depth of the two prints, not in a hurry but taking his time.

Alex traveled several hundred yards across the cleared area before crossing the man's track again. This time the track was just before a pile of brush. The grass had been crushed where an individual had rested and watched the cabin for some time. The crushed grass and brush had sprung back to about half of its normal height. The sitting area was about 250 yards from the cabin and outbuildings. Alex didn't find any more footprints as such, but a small trace of a passage from the pasture into the nearby woods was evident. Someone had been there and had been curious; and it looked as if they had remained for the better part of a day. Alex mounted, returned to the buildings, unsaddled, brushed down and watered his mount, then placed him in the corral with the other horses. Alex decided to alert the other men when they were away from Poinsettia. After briefly describing what he had seen, Alex said,

"No sense in alarming the girl at this point. We men just need to be alert to anything out of the ordinary for awhile." And with that he headed for the cabin.

Storm Cloud lay on his back behind the fallen chestnut tree and watched the stars in the indigo sky overhead. Two days ago he had lain in the clearing near the newly erected buildings of the white people and watched for an entire day. No one ever returned but they had to be nearby. Two of the buildings still bore traces of recent construction. He had considered entering the buildings but the fear of leaving sign in the dusty barren ground around the structures changed his mind. Early the next morning he began his trek to the southwest. He would return at a later time and see if the white occupants had returned. He looked down at his mangled right hand. Four fingers were missing from his knuckles upward. He scowled. Storm Cloud had an immense hatred of the whites...and then there was the matter of his missing white horse.

The trees fell quickly to the axes swung by Alex, Tobias, and Herman the German. By the end of the third day the three men had cut, limbed, and with the wagon team, dragged three dozen logs down to the site of the new bunkhouse. Herman was proving that his huge size didn't overshadow his strength. His muscular ability sped the work forward. As soon as the threesome had moved the last log down from the forest, Herman hitched the team to the wagon, drove the wagon down to the creek bed and began loading rock for the fireplace and chimney.

Meanwhile, Alex straddled the first log. Using a foot long adz, he began hewing the log so that it would have a reasonably flat surface on an upper and lower side. He swung the adz overhead and pulled the tool toward him after it bit into the logs surface. It was a wide log, so it took two swings to drag each chip away. Then he stepped backward and swung again, each time letting the adz bite into the log between his legs. In a matter of minutes, he was ready to rotate the log and repeat the process.

Tobias had marked out the length of the structure and was digging the footing for the fireplace now.

Posey called from the cabin. "Hey, I've supper ready. Come on and wash up! Yell to Herman to come on as well."

Herman drove the wagon back. He unhitched, watered, and corralled the team. Alex and Tobias stowed their tools in the barn. Alex grinned at the others as they washed up and said.

"Don't dawdle. She's just feisty enough now to throw it out if we're not there to eat when she fills the plates. And I don't know about you two, but I could eat a hoss right about now. My belly's rubbing my backbone!"

"Ach! It is so. Our wee lassie yells to komm her, we better come on or there won't be anything to eat. Herman threw his towel at Billy and took off running toward the doorway. Billy was right behind him!

CHAPTER NINE

Jessie McGregor

Jessie McGregor held a firebrand in his right hand and stared at the single-story log house and its dog run porch that had been his home for four years. Now here it was in the first months of the year 1818 and he was starting over...and all because of Abe Upton who couldn't hold his liquor. A week ago, only seven short days past, Upton had walked over to Jessie's mule drawn wagon when it was hitched at the post of Nob's Gristmill, reached into the wagon bed and helped himself to a fresh jug of the product of Jessie's still.

Upton uncorked the jug, stood back from the wagon, waved at Jessie, took a healthy swig of the crock's contents, and yelled at Jessie "Damn fine corn, Jess. I might pay you sometime!" and faking a salute, turned and started across the clearing that fronted the gristmill.

"Stop, Abe Upton! You can't just take my products without paying. You owe me two bits. So, hold it right there." McGregor yelled.

"Nah, got no money now, Jess." Abe turned back toward Jessie. "But damn fine shine. I can sample it for you anytime." He took another swig of the savory brew and belched. That's when Jess drew his horse pistol from his belt, took deliberate aim, and fired. The massive .50 caliber lead ball struck Upton right above the left eye and removed the top of his head. His body jerked. He fell stiff and straight as a log backward to the ground. The jug broke on impact. That was seven days ago, just seven days.

Then, two days later following the incident, the Burke County Constable and his deputy rode over to Jessie McGregor's farm. The constable had helloed the house before dismounting. Jessie opened the door and met Constable Jack Green as he stepped onto the cabin's porch.

"Howdy, Constable Green." Jessie was amicable.

So was the constable. Green came straight to the point of the visit and spoke in a sensible tone of voice.

"Jessie, we all know that you shot ol' Abe Upton. No doubt you had reason to. He was a thief, we all knew him for what he was, a thief, bully, and a braggart. But you pulled trigger on the scoundrel. We all agree, no one faults you. That is, except his kinfolk over near the Burke County seat at Morganton. The Magistrate wants you to appear before him in 10 days. He sent me to summons you and right here's the complaint. I guess you'll have to own up in court to shooting Abe. A bunch of us saw it happen though, and we'll testify to his behavior and why he was shot. All in your favor of course..that is ceptin' for his kin and what they might say."

"Well, Jack," Jess scratched his chin. "I aimed for his nose, and I hit right thar!" And Jess jabbed his forefinger just above the constable's left eye. "I shore can't argue with the complaint, can I? Seems a long way to go though, considering that its 30 miles to Morganton from here on Rackett Creek, and just for shooting a thieving skellum!"

Jack nodded in the affirmative. "Ol Abe was a scoundrel, that's true. And tis a day's ride to Morganton. Hate that for you, sure do. Guess you'd better go though, seeing as how we're a county and all now. Folks will sort of expect you to show up and follow the law, don'tcha know." And with that, Jack Green remounted, tossed a wave at Jessie, turned his horse, and he and his deputy rode off toward the ford at the Antley and Rackett Creek junction.

That was just five days ago. Jessie stared at his home a minute more and then tossed the flaming torch through the open doorway, turned about and walked to the barn. Behind him, the flames crawled up the wall of the house and onto the rough shingled roof. Soon the entire structure was engulfed in flame.

Jessie occupied himself in the barn that afternoon and into the night arranging his packs of food, his possibles, and the few tools that he planned to carry along on his journey. Weary, he crawled into a pile of hay and fell asleep. He awoke at daybreak and spent the morning sifting through the cabin's ashes for the blacksmith forged nails he had used in the cabin's construction. He gathered all the nails that could be found, wrapped the lot in an oil cloth poke, and placed them in the pack he had strapped on the tethered pack horse earlier in the morning. He strode over to the corral and saddled his favorite mount, the black stallion, removed the gate bars from the corral and shooed the remaining two horses out of the corral, freeing them.

Afterward he checked the priming on his long rifle and his belt pistol. Then, he stepped over to the large hickory tree that stood in front of the cabin's remains. Drawing his belt knife, Jessie boldly carved the initials GTT into the tree's trunk.

"Gone to Texas" he thought. "That's all anyone needs to know if they come looking. Gone to Texas, GTT." Jess placed the long rifle in the scabbard on the right side of the black's saddle's rigging and mounted. He spurred lightly and trotted down the road, forded Antley Creek, and headed west toward the setting sun.

By noon the following day, Jessie was on the valley trail below the mountain known to all as Black Dome. By nightfall on day three he rode up to the tavern and combination trading post that stood beside the log courthouse of Asheville, North Carolina. He dismounted and stretched, drew his long rifle from its scabbard, and cradled it in the crook of his left arm, barrel pointing rearward. He stepped up onto the tavern's porch, pushed the right double door open, and looked inside. The tavern was deserted except for four card players at a table near the far end of the tavern's bar. Jessie strode over to the bar. The barkeep approached.

"What'll it be, sire?" He asked Jessie.

"Have you a room to let, and a pot of coffee in the room?"

The barkeep answered, "Aye, three bits and we'll stable your horse."

"I have my mount and a pack animal. And I'll water and feed them. You have grain and hay, I should hope."

"Make it four bits, stranger, and I'll include the fodder for both animals. I'll send a man for your gear and have it placed in your room.".

Jessie dropped two shiny United States quarter dollar coins on the counter. "Throw in a tub of hot water and a bar of soap and those are yours. Alright?"

The bartender nodded and motioned to an older black man seated behind the far end of the bar. "Moses, go with the stranger and show him to the barn, help him get his animals fed and watered, and then tote his gear up to the room at the top of the stairs. Be quick now."

Jessie laid a hand on the black man's shoulder. "Go easy, Moses, It's been a long day for us both, I suspect. Just show me the way and then take my gear to the room and watch over it until I get there. I'll take care of my animals." The black man nodded with a slight grin and headed out the door. Jessie followed him. The card players continued their game undisturbed.

The next morning a refreshed Jessie saddled up and leading his packhorse, headed toward the French Broad River and the mountain gap to Knoxville, one hundred and sixteen miles farther west. By nightfall the trail's altitude had increased, and the air was cooler. Jessie made a dry camp on the Tennessee side of the mountains and slept near a blazing fire.

A grunting sound aroused him from slumber. A wet nose thrust against his cheek followed by a chorus of grunts and squeals fetched him from his bedroll. Grasping his rifle and cocking the hammer and then taking a step backward from the animals that surrounded him, he aimed at the largest one.

"Hold fire, mountain man, hold your fire! Them's friendly pigs and I'm driving 'em to market. Hold fire!" A shaggy haired and lanky man with a long grey beard stepped into the firelight.

"Didn't mean to disturb you, but the pigs, they ran toward the firelight before I could get in front of the wee herd and head them off. But they're friendly pigs, they won't harm ye. I 'ave eaten part of one already and saved some of its bacon. You want some? It's shore tasty meat cause I raise 'em good, my pigs, I shore do."

The pigs clustered around the legs of both men. "See here now, I'm known as Dolphus, Dolphus the pig man."

"Well, Dolphus, I'm Jess, um, Jess Gregg." Jessie thought before giving out his real name of McGregor. "If you'll get these varmints away from my camp, I'll stir up a pot of coffee and a cold biscuit or two in exchange for some of that bacon you mentioned."

After eating, the conversation turned to the immediate. Dolphus asked, "Where bouts you headed, Jess?"

Jessie pointed west. "That way. West. Texas maybe! You?"

"Taking them hawgs to the Asheville market. Get myself a grub stake for the next couple o' months. What'cha going to Texas for?"

Jess was quiet for a moment before speaking. "More land, maybe. Here tell it's almost free. The Mexican government has started giving tracts of land to renown American business leaders who in turn are selling it cheap, like 6 bits for an acre, or so I heard tell."

Dolphus sipped his coffee and grunted. "Hope that you like Indians some. Word from over past Knoxville is that some of the Northern tribes from the Ohio Valley ain't real friendly, been drifting into Tennessee. Suspicion is that the British are still sending agents out amongst the redskins to stir them up. They ain't forgotten Mad Anthony Wayne's defeating them at Fallen Timbers back near 25 years ago. Guess they'll always be angry, and the British too! Especially after Jackson kicked them outa New Orleans back in '14.

Thought I'd turn southwest just past Knoxville. Maybe travel down the old Warrior's Path toward the edge of the Cherokee Territory around Titsohill, that's a Cherokee trading town, or so I've been told. American name now is Wattstown."

"What in heaven's name is there?" queried Dolphus. "Never heard tell of such a place myself."

"Long about the time I got my first good corn crop in, about four years ago, a black fellow, freedman from down in South Carolina, had stopped in the Globe Valley looking for work. Seems he had started for Tejas, or Texas, not long after the end of the Revolutionary War. Got stranded in lower Florida and was attempting to start west again but by a different route. Came through the mountains dodging the slavers. Name was Thaddeus, Thaddeus Prentiss. He told me about a Cherokee trading town in Alabama territory called Titsohill where the Cherokee and the White Stick Creek Indians lived peaceably. He had thought to go there first, then on to Tejas. Thought maybe I might follow his directions some. Might even meet up with him along the way. Who knows. He seemed to be a straight-forward kinda man. He had traveled a good bit since leaving the coast of South Carolina and moving on to Florida and the territory of Alabama. Only been a couple or three years now since he left my farm, didn't have no work then for a hired hand. What about you after you sell them hogs?"

"Wal, I ha'int thought too much on it, after selling this batch, I guess. I'm just sort of tired of messing with hogs. They've sorta have a stink about them after awhile, you know." Dolphus cleared his throat. "Appreciate the coffee and biscuit. Guess I'll start them pigs up and head on over to the Asheville settlement."

Jess tossed the remains of the coffee pot out and put the pot and cups back into his pack. "Hope you get a good price for the critters. And thanks for the trail warning about the redskins. See you!"

The two men parted and headed their separate ways, one yelling to his pigs, the other leading his pack horse down the mountain trail west toward Knoxville.

Soon Jessie couldn't hear the 'hoooo...piggy....hooooo' wailing anymore. The forest solitude enveloped him, drawing him into the mountain fastness.

CHAPTER TEN

The Bear

The south side of the trail overlooked a shallow rocky gorge. The northern slope of the trail was a forest of 150-foot tulip popular trees that rose upward creating a towering hillside. Jessie rode west along the defined trail. The floor of the gorge harbored a slow-moving stream that followed the gradual descent of the terrain.

The mountain air was crisp and fresh. As the morning progressed the wind began to shift slightly. It blew more from the west now. Jessie pulled up his horse and swung his right leg up onto the saddle's swell, taking his ease for a few moments. The black stallion pawed the ground and huffed, stretched his forelegs out, and made water. The pack horse snorted and stepped left, turning sideways.

"Scent of smoke in the air." Jessie mused. "Just smell it off and on. Let's be sharp, hoss, good possibility something lies ahead." He nudged the horse with the heel of his boot. He and his horses moved steadily along the forested trail. Half an hour had soon passed, and the trail began a descent toward the floor of the gorge. Soon the trail leveled and turned southward. The gorge walls dropped away and the stream bed and rocky floor of the gorge became much wider. One long stretch of a solid rock cliff face stretched into a v-shaped cliff on the left side of the wider trail. A clear waterfall dropped from the top of the cliff down to the stream bed below and formed a pool 100 feet long by 60 feet wide. A grass slope lay to the south of the creek and stretched along the stream bottom down the widened gorge. Seven Indian lodges were scattered on the grassy slope with a larger one near the pond. Two camp dogs lay near a small cook fire. A suspended iron pot hung from a tripod above the fire. The camp was quiet. The few visible inhabitants seemed to be engaged in normal chores. None appeared to be warlike or aware of his presence as he passed above the camp. The camp dogs never even barked as he rode above and past the small gathering of lodges.

Jess dismounted and led his animals nearer the hillside of the trail where they would be less likely seen from the bottom of the gorge. Quietly, stealthily, he followed the trail over the top of the falls and rode past the descending trace that led off from the main trail. Just on the far side of the falls and the ford, the way led off through a heavy stand of spruce trees. The fallen spruce needles that covered the ground muffled the sound of his horses' passage. After traveling a mile or more on foot, he remounted and moved faster along the trail away from the small Indian encampment.

Maple and black gum trees began to displace the spruce forest. Trailside brush and berry vine clusters began to crowd the hardwood forested floor. The tangled vines held early spring berries. Strange though, Jess didn't hear many bird calls in that area as he passed.

The sow bear had slept well during the winter. Stored fat had kept her warm. Now, hibernation over, her drooping belly ached with hunger. She growled softly as she pushed through the brush and clustered berry vines. She pulled berry laden vines toward her and scooped the fruit into her mouth. She caught an unusual scent. It smelled of horse sweat. She stood up on her hind legs, twisting her body about, scenting the air, mindful of the unexplained smell. Satisfied that there wasn't a threat, she dropped back to all fours and began feeding again.

Jess heard a soft rustle of brush just to his left in a thicket on the slope of the hill.

"Not an Indian. Sounds too heavy." Jessie thought. He eased the long rifle out of its scabbard and swung it across the saddle. Cautious now and wary, his eyes scanned left and right along the sides of the trail. He thought that he heard a twig pop not far behind him. The pack horse jerked its head up as something moved again on the left. Jessie spurred his mount and trotted ahead, distancing himself from the unseen. Two hundred yards farther down the trail, he pulled rein, dismounted, and tethered the two horses. He stepped over to the right side of the trail and quietly eased back the way he had ridden for about 30 yards.

There was a soft woof or grunt from a berry thicket to the left of the forest trail. Jess swung the rifle to his shoulder, cocking the hammer in the same fluid motion. He saw the black bear stand up on its hind legs in the middle of the berry patch. Jessie looked down his rifle's barrel and drew a sight on the huge beast. The bear turned slightly to face this new threat, growled harshly, dropped to all fours, and charged out of the thicket toward the mountaineer. Jessie waited for three seconds. The she-bear hit the trail's clearing, roared, and reared up on her hind legs. She lunged toward the human, mouth wide open, roaring, and waving her forepaws with her claws unsheathed. Jess's trigger pull was instantaneous with the bear's upright charge. The heavy caliber ball spun the animal off course. Jess switched the rifle to his left hand and drew his horse pistol from his waist belt. The bear regained its footing and charged again. Jessie leveled the pistol and fired as the bear closed the distance to 10 yards.

The bear stumbled and nosed to the ground, sliding, trying to regain its footing, still attempting to reach the shooter. The horses were frantic; lunging, pulling, and rearing at their tethers. Quick as a flash, Jessie dropped the empty guns on the ground and drew his belt knife.

The bear clawed the ground with one forepaw dragging himself forward, still intent on the attack. Jessie ran to the left of the fallen omnivore and straddled the animal's back, leaned forward against the flat top of the bear's head, and plunged his long knife blade into the animal's neck beneath its jaw. The man shoved the knife through the bear's thick hide, jerked the knife blade forward and ripped it out of the animal's neck, severing the animal's arteries. Blood gushed from the wound and from the bear's open mouth. The bear emitted a low groan and collapsed. The attack was over.

Jessie drew a breath and stood, shaken. "That's a big bear, close to 500 pounds or so, I'd think. Too close a scrape. Could be me lying there instead of that varmint. Sure would be a lot of meat if I were still on the farm. I sure hope she was feeding alone." With the thought of a possible second bear in mind, Jess picked up his rifle, sat the rifle's butt on the toe of his boot, uncorked his powder horn, and charged the rifle, reloaded with a patched ball, and rammed it home. After charging the frizzen, he leaned the rifle against a tree and reloaded his pistol.

"Seems shameful to let all this meat go to waste. I'll take a chunk of backstrap for today's meal along with enough for tomorrow. Guess the buzzards can have the rest." He finished catching his breath then bent to the task of removing some of the meat from the bear carcass. He dropped the hunk of fresh bear meat in a linen sack and hung it from his saddle horn. After calming the horses, he climbed into the black's saddle and rode farther down the mountain toward the valley below.

Three days later, long about noon, Jessie noticed a tendril of smoke rising above the trees as he crested a high hill. He led his pack animals and rode toward the smoke. Emerging from the dark forest interior, he rode into a pasture clearing that fronted four substantial log buildings.

"Looks like some settlers, hoss." Jessie spurred the black onward. He noticed a man standing in the doorway of the center building and reined his horse in that direction. Jess dismounted in front of a hitching post and draped his reins over the post's bar.

He stretched and faced the man in the doorway. "Came over the mountains from North Carolina and down Tennessee way. Can I approach?"

"Aye, stranger, and welcome if you mean no harm!"

"None meant. Any chance of food and drink?" Jessie inquired.

"Sure nuff, welcome to Poinsettia Springs Trading Post on Commons Creek. We can offer some food and drink. Also, supplies for sale or barter. Come on in, first cup of juice is on the house."

CHAPTER ELEVEN

Water Barrel

Another man was watching the four buildings that comprised the Poinsettia Springs Trading Post. Storm Cloud rubbed his fingerless right hand and watched as the rider that he had trailed for the past three days dismounted and conversed with the Post's proprietor. The Indian had heard the two gunshots that had echoed through the mountain fastness when Jessie had dispatched the bear earlier. Curious, he had traveled along the trail from the Indian village at the water fall until he found the dead bear.

He observed the amount of meat removed from the fresh kill. It was only enough for one or two men. He also cut some meat from the freshly killed bear and continued to follow the horse tracks along the mountain's slope. Now here he was, concealed by a tumble of large boulders on the hillside above the four log buildings. He had been here before. That was several seasons past. Then there had only been three buildings, not four.

He watched as a young woman exited one of the buildings with a sack and approached a half dozen horses in a nearby corral. Storm Cloud's eyes opened wider in surprise. One of the corralled horses was solid white with a black stocking forefoot. He recognized the mare. She had been his before the day almost six winters ago when she had been stolen and he had awakened to the pain in his right hand from his missing fingers.

Storm Cloud removed a piece of jerky from his pouch, placed it in his mouth, and chewed thoughtfully as he observed the woman graining the corralled horses. He remembered the joy of riding the mare, she had varying gaits, all smooth.

"She old now." The Indian chewed and thought reflectively. "Probably no long rides, not fast anymore. Still, she is my horse. Not belong to whites. How come her to be here? Now, at this place. That last ride, halted at big rock. Heard children sounds, girl like. See white girl look over top of rock. I looked down when stone hit ground. Then just as I look up again, hit in head. Wake up, my fingers gone. Horse gone too!" He watched the white woman as she fed the horses. The white mare trotted over to her, nickering, then nuzzled the woman's outstretched hand.

Storm Cloud gritted his teeth. "Could woman have been child on cliff? Get horse back when the moon comes up later tonight. Then see if woman follows!" The Indian fingered his knife hilt and scowled. He lay down on his back behind the rocky pile, closed his eyes, and slept.

The whiskey was smooth and balanced in flavor without the harshness of many of the tavern whiskeys served on the frontier. Jessie savored the beverage's taste.

"That's a well distilled whiskey, sir. Your work?"

'Aye, tis. I learned the craft from my Da. He was a Carolina landsman, true to his Scots heritage, he was." Alex Avery grinned and lifted the jug from the shelf behind him. "Care for another dram?"

"Where in Carolina, North or South? I hail from the Carolina's too, and aye, I would enjoy another dram, make it three."

Alex nodded and poured the shot of whiskey. "I'm from the coastal forest of South Carolina, Hickory Grove, near the river town of Kingston on the Waccamaw River. My Da and

Mother owned a large acreage farm there. Brother and Sister have it now. I hankered to travel a bit, see the untamed wilderness. You, whereabouts do you hail from?"

"Rode down from the mountains near the settlements of Watauga, particularly a small community called The Globe on the John's River in North Carolina. I too had a farm there. Got my tail feathers ruffled near there one time at a new town named Morganton. There were those who thought I should answer for my response to the ruffling. So, I burned my cabin and barn, signed a tree with my knife by marking it GTT, and lit out. Here I am, now, drinking this fine whiskey, and still got a ways to go to get to Texas."

Alex poured himself a shot. "Often thought of Texas. Traded some furs with a trapper last month. He spoke of a man name of Austin, I think, yes, Stephen Austin. Claimed he was starting a settlement on the Brazos River a bit inland from the Gulf of Mexico, called it, what was it, oh, yeah, called it San Felipe de Austin. Austin was talking about recruiting about 1500 families to make up this town. Seems he had asked the Mexican Governor for an 11-million-acre landgrant. The trapper seemed to think Austin had got it started a couple of years ago, along about 1821 or so. Said that he was offering prospective settlers 4,428 acres for a service fee of $ 60.00."

"That's a lot of land." Jessie spoke over his glass.

"Sure nuff, but I understood him to say that around 170 acres or so was to be farming land for corn and vegetables, and such. The rest was grazing land for cattle and sheep."

"Get there by crossing the river by ship I guess, probably boarding the vessel over in Louisiana?" Jessie asked.

"That would likrly be easier and safer than going overland, hear tell there's some rough Injuns out that away." Alex wiped a small wet spot from the bar.

Poinsettia saw the strange horse tethered in front of the trading post. She placed the remaining fodder in the horses' feed trough in the corral and strode at a rapid pace toward the post thinking that Alex might need assistance in filling orders.

She stepped through the trading post's doorway. Blinded now by having been in the brilliant sunlight, it took several moments for her eyes to adjust to the shadowy interior of the building. She heard Alex's familiar voice and saw his form behind the counter. But a taller figure was on the customer side of the counter, a taller soft-spoken man. Gradually her eyes adjusted to the darker surroundings. She moved toward the end of the counter and joined Alex, whispering softly in his ear that she would lend a hand if he needed some help in filling an order.

She waited...and glanced up shyly at the new arrival. He had a bronzed tanned face with a friendly countenance. Even a smile that beamed in her direction. He touched his forefinger to his hat brim.

"Afternoon, Miss. My name's Jessie, Jessie Gregg. My friends call me Jess. Hope that you will, too."

Warmth flooded her face. Never in her life had she ever dreamed that a man would notice her as a woman. He had tipped his hat, or at least fingered the brim, and asked her to be his friend.

"Aye, I guess that could be, uh, Mr. Jess Gregg." She stammered, thinking 'What's wrong with me. I've no' had trouble speaking with strangers before. What is going on?' Aye, I guess so, sir." She looked down at the counter.

"And your name, Miss. You do have one, I presume."

"Of course I do! It's Poinsettia, Posey. My friends call me Posey. Maybe I shall let you call me Posey also."

"I pray so, Miss Poinsettia. It is Miss, and not Mistress, I trust, nay, I hope." Jessie smiled. "A lovely name to go with such a rare beauty in an out of the way frontier borderland!"

Alex turned around and placed the whiskey flagon back on the shelf, chuckling to himself. Never had he or any of the others on the post's grounds seen Posey at a loss for words. The lass was always strong willed and quick tempered. But something had just transpired. Alex regained his self control and smothered his mirth before turning back to the counter.

"Well, friend Jessie. Glad you enjoyed the wee taste of the spirits. What can I help thee with today?" Turning to Posey he said, "Posey, how about you fetch over a pad and quill, we'll start a bill of goods for friend Jessie."

Billy Rudd whistled loudly to gain the attention of the six horses in the corral, dipped a wooden bucket into the rain barrel, leaned over the fence, and poured the water into the corral's water trough. The day had been long and laborious. Watering stock was the last organized chore of the day. The sun was near setting, lower in the western sky, and cooler. He drew another bucket of water from the chest-high rain barrel and stepped forward to empty the bucket into the corral's horse trough. The sunlight formed a shadow in front of him, one that looked like a head with a pointed feather. "Odd shape, that." Billy mused to himself.

Something tapped him on the shoulder as he straightened up. He saw the single eagle feather in the scalp lock before noticing the Indian's grinning face and the extended bow pointed at him. Before Billy could complete his turn or yell, Storm Cloud dropped the bow and body slammed Billy against the corral fence, picked him up, turned him upside down and dropped him headfirst into the water barrel.

The unexpected immersion forced water up Billy's nose. Gagging, he was struggling to right himself within the barrel's watery confines.

Meanwhile, Storm Cloud slung his bow and ran to the corral gate and swung it open. The six horses started toward him.

He flung up his arms as the white mare neared, rushed to her side, grasped the horse's mane, and swung onto its back. Guiding the horse with his knees, he rode through the corral gate, across the broad clearing, and toward the sheltering forest. Storm Cloud yelled a triumphant war cry and shook his fist in the air. He had just counted coup on an enemy white man and recovered his stolen mare! His medicine was strong. He sang his war song as he galloped away from the white man's trading post.

Billy was drowning. He shoved and pushed against the wooden sides of the rain barrel. It began to tilt and teeter. He pushed harder, rocking the barrel back and forth. It was getting difficult to hold his breath. The barrel tilted farther and fell over, bursting as it impacted the ground, spilling its water and Billy into the dusty yard of the trading post.

Billy was yelling and struggling to regain his footing in the mud. "Alex, Tobias, Herman. Indians; they're stealing our horses. Bring a gun. Get over here, where are you people?" Billy struggled to his feet and started for the trading post's front door when it burst open and a strange man with a long black rifle charged out, followed by Alex and Poinsettia. The stranger glanced at Billy. Billy pointed at the fleeing Indian. Jessie swung his rifle up and quickly sighted on the distant galloping horseman. The rifle cracked. The white horse appeared to stumble, regained its footing, and galloped out of sight into the forest.

Posey ran past Jessie and swung up on his saddled horse, wheeled the animal about, and raced across the clearing toward the loose horses. "I'll catch them!" she cried.

Tobias was running across a plowed field toward the group. He altered his direction toward the loose horses to block their path. Together he and Posey herded the five horses back into their enclosure.

Alex stared at his bedraggled cousin. "You look a mite damp. You okay, William? How'd you get in the rain barrel?"

"There was an Indian. I didn't see him until I turned after something tapped me on the shoulder. He slammed me into the corral. Knocked the wind out of me. Strong, he was. He picked me up and flung me into the water barrel."

Jessie spoke up. "Was there more Indians or just the one man?"

Billy shook his head no. "Just him, I think. At least that's all I saw. I don't know what he was doing here. I don't think there was anyone with him."

Tobias walked over and stood alongside Alex. "I saw him, Injun, he Storm Cloud. Remember, man who Poinsettia dropped the rock on, came for his horse, I reckon." Tobias slapped Billy on the shoulder. "You lucky feller, you. He only counted coup. I saw it. Injun way of saying 'Could'da had your scalp, white man'. He hurt you anywhere else, Billy Rudd?"

"No, Tobias, other than being wet. And mad about being ambushed or couped or whatever you called it, I'm not hurt. I guess all the others are okay, Posey, and you, Alex? What about the German? Where's Herman?"

Alex pointed past the bunkhouse as the door to the privy swung open and Herman came out, pulling a suspender into place on his shoulder.

The German trudged toward the group. "Ich bin hier? Was is passiert? What's happened?" Herman looked questioningly at the group.

The tension drained instantly from all of them. They laughed. All but Jessie. He just stared, thinking it was a good thing for the redskin that he hadn't attempted to put the giant Herman in the water barrel!

Alex glanced at those gathered around the wet Billy Rudd. "Hells Bells, what do y'all think, should we mount up and go after him. Looks like he got one of our horses, appears to be the white mare of Posey's."

"Not necessary," Billy scowled. "He could have killed me or bushwhacked any of us. I say let him go and keep the horse. She was getting past her prime anyway."

Tobias nodded in agreement. "Probably was Storm Cloud's tracks we saw some time back, Alex. He watched for a spell before attempting coup, I betcha. Let em be. Now he feel like his medicine strong. Might be harder to kill if we catch him right away. Might be another time, a better time later. Less cocky injun then." Tobias looked at Posey. "Okay with you or you want us go get the horse?"

"Tobias, we can trade for more horses anytime. The horse served its purpose years ago for my sister and me. Mona's gone, I'm here with y'all; I say let him be. Why take a chance. Let's get cleaned up. We have a guest. Calls for fried chicken. Herman, I need a fat hen while I make preparations and mix a batter for some biscuits."

Herman grinned at Posey. "Ja, I go kill das huhn, the chicken. Sounds gut!"

CHAPTER TWELVE

Table Talk

Poinsettia drew the curtain closed that separated her living quarters from Alex's room. The other men now maintained quarters in the new bunkhouse. Posey filled the washbasin on the shelf near the end of her bed. The cool water felt good as she washed her face, hands, and arms.

"Why did she act so giddy and irresponsible whenever she was near this stranger calling himself Jessie?" Posey mumbled to herself as she peered into the mirror Alex had fastened to the wall above the basin's shelf.

She had never in her life here on earth wanted a man to notice her like she yearned for this North Carolina vagabond's attention. Posey patted her hair down in the back after brushing it vigorously.

"My frock's still fresh enough. Guess I'll go and began the preparations for the meal now."

She brushed the curtain aside and bumped into Jessie. His back was turned to her.

"Excuse me, sir." She ducked her head and rushed to the table she used for food preparation, pulled out a large wooden trencher from the cupboard, and placed it on the table. Then she opened a small flour cask and using a horn scoop, she placed the flour in the trencher and added salt and pepper somewhat liberally, all of the time feeling like her face was on fire.

Herman the German shouldered his bulky body through the cabin door waving a plucked and cleaned chicken carcass. "Here ist das huhn, das chicken." And he handed it to Posey.

It took a little over an hour for Posey to cut, bread, and fry the chicken for their meal. She boiled potatoes as a side dish for the fried chicken. It seemed that no time had passed before she called them to the table.

The German, Billy, Tobias, Alex, and the handsome stranger Jessie found seats around the table. Jessie pulled a chair out for Posey and stood until she was seated.

Talk among them during and after the meal centered around the uncharted western lands beyond the frontier commonly called the Indian Territory.

"What lies between here and the big River? That's what I'd like to know before heading out that way." Jessie looked at the group expectantly.

Billy pointed his fork at Tobias. "Tob's been there once. Tell us about what's over the mountain, Tobias."

"Lot of trees, big trees, 'specially along the western side of our mountain. Up above us, three white waters come together, form one big river, Warrior river, that flows from the hills down to the big salt water. Headwater is very old river, older than time, formed with the mountains so my ancestors say, my Grandfather tell me that river was there from the beginning of time. Two other white waters join it in rush to large water. Rough going up there, all the way down Warrior river. Grandfather say the big river guarded by spirit warriors, keep current swiftl on purpose. You must cross these waters to get to the big muddiest river, the one you call Mississippi."

"White folks have gone there, though, surely. Or we wouldn't have heard so much about Tejas. Must be a path, a way through the wilderness." Jess looked across the table at Poinsettia. "And if white men went there, you know that they didn't go alone; bound to have taken some ladies along. And livestock."

Posey felt her face suddenly heat up. The stranger was watching her, waiting for an expression, her thoughts. Her tongue felt thick. She knew how to speak.

"What is wrong with me?" She thought. Posey pushed a wisp of her hair back into place.

"I think, Mr. Jessie, that many have attempted to trek through that wilderness. Some have succeeded. We have some customers, trappers, who bring their hides that they have taken from the animals in those forests to trade with us. They never linger long though. Its almost as if there is an unseen force always calling them back to the trees, doesn't it, Alex?"

"Aye, Posey. And they claim that there's plenty of game on the far side of the mountains, buffalo, elk and deer, beaver too. And plenty of Indians. Some noble, like the Cherokees and the White Stick Creeks. But some like the Chickasaw and the Red Sticks as well as some others, they aren't so friendly. And a few Iroquois filter down occasionally from Kentucky, they say.

Last year, one of the trappers' parties, they travel in groups, you know, a few to clean and prep the hides, some to keep camp, and the others to hunt and trap the animals for their pelts. Anyway, early last fall, a group's camp was raided while the hunters were minding their traps and chasing game. The Indians, Chickasaw and some Iroquois, captured two of the camp keepers alive. Those two that were captured, the trappers told me, might have lasted two days once they reached the main encampment before they died.

One of the trappers told Billy and me that they had trailed the Indian war party for almost a week when they found their deserted campsite. The remains of the two captives were still bound to trees where fires were built beneath the trappers' feet. Their flesh had been torn from their arms and upper thighs.

They had been emasculated, their private parts cut out, and their tongues removed before being scalped, so it appeared."

"Aye, Alex. These are some bad people, much to be feared and not taken too lightly." Billy nodded. "What Alex hasn't said is that some of the group of trappers, the ones that got back whole, have refused to go that way again, traveling farther south this time."

"Definitely not a suitable or safe place for womenfolk unless the party of travelers was large enough to cause the Indians to hesitate in warlike action. And yet, interestingly, we know that the settlements just like the one down on Coosa Creek, Alabama Town, the settlers there just keep pushing on west. And then there's that Austin fellow and his settlement across the Mississippi in Tejas that keeps sending invitations for folks to join him....and some do, I hear. Pass the biscuits, please." Alex asked politely.

Jessie smiled at Poinsettia. "Miss Posey, that was some fine chicken and a scrumptious meal. Best I've had since I left home. I think I'll retire to the bunkhouse and my blankets now, and wish all y'all a good night. I'm thinking of getting an early start in the morning and ride down to that Alabama Town you mentioned. See what kind of news they have about the way west. I'd like to come back this way in a few days and visit again, Miss Poinsettia, if its okay with you."

"It would be our pleasure, kind sir. Wouldn't it, Alex." Posey finally smiled at Jessie.

He winked at her, pushed his chair back from the table, and stood up.

"Good night then. And count on it, Missy, I'll return."

Tobias stood as well. "Good meal, Posey. Thanks. I turn in now too."

The two men walked to the bunkhouse. Tobias spoke first. "Mr. Jessie, been thinking about that injun Storm Cloud that you shot at today sure."

Jessie nodded. "Yeah."

"Sure have. You know, I think that you hit him or the horse. Likely the horse, it stumbled. I saw." Tobias said.

"Wasn't sure, Tobias. I thought so too. And?"

"Well, you talk about leaving tomorrow, going down to Alabama Town. I think I go with you. Maybe, just maybe, you and I hunt that bad Injun on the way if we cross his trail, what you think?"

"Tobias, I'm in agreement. I don't like leaving things undone. And if that man thinks that he got the goods on y'all and got away, chances are he'll come back and try again. Let's see if we can even the score. If we succeed, we can tell the others when we return."

"Alex, he might not agree if we tell now. So let's go prepare for the hunt tomorrow. Be sure and replace the powder in your horn. There's a keg in the bunkhouse. Get some."

Tobias Walking Horse and Jessie Gregg had saddled up early. They were on their way leading one pack horse long before daylight. At the far edge of the clearing, Tobias dismounted and searched the edge of the field on foot until he crossed the tracks of the fleeing Storm Cloud. Tobias's youthful training as a Cherokee brave enabled him to quickly ascertain Storm Cloud's direction of travel. He remounted and pointed toward the forest.

"He's headed toward the valley beyond the mountain, probably a village there." He urged his mount forward and led the way into the dark forest as the new day dawned, lighting the field they had just left.

Jessie turned in his saddle, looked back toward the faraway cluster of buildings, and thought of the girl, nay, woman, called Posey, Poinsettia. He faced front and trotted after Tobias. Both men were of the same mindset. Their intent was to end the threat of any future attack and return alive.

They rode through the day, stopping twice to rest and water the animals. Storm Cloud's trail faded in and out for the first 10 miles. After that, it appeared that disguising his direction of travel became less important to him. The two men made better time now, gaining on their quarry after they crested the mountains.

"Ho!, hah! Ho!" The shout from the Indian as he stepped into the forest clearing halted Storm Cloud's progress and startled his horse.

"Why are you in my way?" Storm Cloud asked in his native tongue.

Three more Indians appeared in the clearing. "You are traveling toward our lodges in some haste. Are you being followed?" The question was asked in the Chickasaw language. "If so, brother, we can help you and are willing."

Storm Cloud dismounted and walked toward them, leading his white mare. The animal limped. Dried blood was visible on her left flank.

"My horse is injured, and yes, there may be followers." Storm Cloud related his version of counting coup and the raid on the trading post. The recounting of the affair excited the other four young men. They had visions of plunder, mayhem, and mighty deeds that could be recounted in their village if they could participate in a similar raid.

"Our brother Storm Cloud is a mighty warrior filled with valor. We should all return to the white man's trading post and have a reckoning for invading our territory and stealing this fine warrior's white horse. His spirit horse! Waugh!" The brave waved a tomahawk over his head. The other three joined in with an impromptu war dance. Storm Cloud grinned and joined the chanting. To him, the idea of another raid on the remote post sounded good. And perhaps revenge for the loss of his fingers was in the offing.

"I'll need a fresh horse. Have you one?"

The leader of the four Indians spoke up. "We have three horses that we have taken from the white man's village in the South. We were taking them back to our village, that way." And he pointed northwest.

"A half day's ride. We can be there by moonrise, rest, eat, sleep, leave your spirit horse there. Ride out at sunrise for the white man's trading post. Make war, count coup, take many scalps. Waugh!"

The five Chickasaws mounted and rode out, leading the white mare and the two other stolen horses.

Two days later, Tobias came to a halt and motioned for Jessie to stop at the edge of a small creek. The creek's rocky bank had been disturbed by the passage of a few riders heading eastward, parallel to the trail they were following, but in a reverse direction.

Tobias stared at the tracks. He knelt on one knee, picked up a clump of disturbed mud, and fingered it, feeling the remaining moisture in the dirt clump. He stood, brushing his hands, and said, "Early this morning, they pass here. Four or six riders, I think. They're headed back out, over the mountain, the way we came! Traveling light too. No pack animals."

"How do you know they don't have pack horses, Tobias?"

"Jessie, weight on pack horses cause deeper tracks. These tracks all the same pretty much. Just riders, no packs. Looks like war party, maybe. Traveling light and fast!"

Jessie removed his hat and scratched his head. "I don't particularly care for that news, Tobias. Might they be headed for y'alls trading post"

"Might be. If so, one of these riders is likely to be Storm Cloud. But not same horse hoof prints we've been following. Might be he could'a changed horses, might be your rifle shot hit horse back when he fled the post."

"That means Posey and the men are going to be surprised. Not good, Tob. You think that's what's about to happen, don't you?" Jessie asked.

"Sure might could be. I think we should head back now, real fast. Water horses now, then we should ride hard, I think!"

Jessie led their horses to the creek's edge and let them drink. He took the canteens from both saddles and filled them on the upstream side of the thirsty mounts. Tobias, after inspecting the tracks a bit more, rejoined him. The two men mounted, wheeled their mounts about, and headed back the way they came.

"Storm Cloud, if it's him, he's leading them back to the post some different trail. Not the one he rode originally. Keep us from crossing their trail. We know different now, make better time if we go back the way we came."

Jessie nodded. "Just ride. Take us the shortest way, Tobias, cross country. We gotta get there before they can do much harm. Time's a'wasting." Jessie spurred his mount.

CHAPTER THIRTEEN

Hostiles

The horses were hidden in the woods facing the corral and the four buildings that comprised the Poinsettia Trading Post. Five Indians, their faces smeared with their personal war colors, watched the four buildings from hiding places on the far side of the small branch that ran near the corral.

The door to the bunkhouse swung open and a large white man stepped through the opening. The four younger braves gasped at the size of the man. Storm Cloud glared at his four companions and grunted softly. "No noise!"

Storm Cloud's face bore the same black painted handprint on both sides of his face in the same manner that he marked his horses. He slowly stood and notched an arrow to his bow with his left hand, placed the four finger stubs remaining on his right hand around the bow string, holding it firmly, and pushed the bow forward by extending his left arm in a move that he had practiced for months following the loss of his fingers. He stood up, arm muscles taunt, bow drawn, and watched the large man amble toward the main cabin.

Herman stopped in front of the cabin door, knocked, and called out "Good Morning". The door opened. Billy stared beyond the German, disbelief in his face. "Inside, Herman, get inside. Now." Herman was slow to respond. Instead, he turned to look behind him.

Storm Cloud's bow string twanged as he loosed the arrow. Storm Cloud screamed his war cry. The missile flew straight, hard and fast, striking the large man just below his ribs on his right side with a loud audible thud.

Herman gasped and lunged through the door. He fell against the prepared kitchen table scattering dishes and food onto the floor. The table crashed to the floor from the injured man's weight. Poinsettia screamed.

Billy yelled. "Indians!"

A windowpane shattered from the impact of a musket ball fired by one of the attackers. Their barbaric yells rent the air. Billy slammed and barred the door. Alex pulled his jerkin over his head, fastened his belt, and rammed his tomahawk's handle into the belt, then grabbed the loaded rifle standing near the bedframe.

Storm Cloud motioned to the four young braves. "Two of you go and burn the building that the big man came out of and run the horses out of that larger building." He pointed at the barn. "Burn it too. Then after we get scalps and the woman, we can burn the rest and take whatever we want. Much dancing tonight. Now, you other two, we will go and attack the cabin. You, with the musket, shoot at the door."

And with that the five warriors ran toward the cluster of buildings.

The barn was easy to fire. After the attacking Indian had chased the horses out, he struck flint to the piled hay. The result was immediate with the flames devouring the dry straw and climbing the barn walls. The other brave had piled brush against the rear wall of the bunkhouse and started a small fire. It soon caught and began to burn the log wall of the shelter.

The two braves rejoined the group in front of the cabin and began firing a musket and shooting arrows from their bows toward the cabin.

Alex rushed to each of the two windows in turn, closed their shutters, and barred them. "Stay away from the windows except to shoot and only shoot through the rifle slots. Posey, did Herman's fall upset the water bucket?"

"No!" Posey shook her head. "It's safe over by the storage cabinet. We have some water, and there's some coffee I had made in the pot on the hearth. It's okay. Nothing has spilled or turned over. Just have to be sparing until this set-to ends and we can draw more water from the well."

Billy was at Herman's side.

The big man's eyes were watering. "Arrow hurts. I think its poking out my back too." Herman rolled over on his left side, gasping in pain as he did.

Billy pulled the man's homespun shirttail up. "Sure is. Grit your teeth, you mad Kraut, I'm gonna break the head off the arrow." Billy used his belt knife to etch around the arrow's shaft. Then he applied pressure and snapped the exposed wood shaft. He showed the arrowhead to Herman and tossed it over onto the hearth.

"Now comes the hard part, Herman. I'm gonna draw the arrow's shaft back through you and flush the wound, then sear it with a red-hot iron to stop the bleeding. Posey, I need your help. Bring over a small pan of boiling water." Billy stood up and stepped to the fireplace and jammed the iron poker into the coals.

Meanwhile, the five attackers had neared the cabin and were yelling. Alex peered through a rifle slit.

"They're yelling like banshees. And they've fired the bunkhouse and barn. There's no way to stop the fire. I'll see if I can sting one of the varmints." Alex extended just the muzzle of his long rifle through the port, took aim, and fired. One of the attackers dropped to the ground clutching his chest. "Happy Hunting Ground for that one." Alex began reloading his rifle.

Storm Cloud ran up to the cabin door and began beating on it with his tomahawk. Alex rammed the rifle through the window's rifle port again and fired at another warrior, striking him in the shoulder and shattering it.

"Billy, leave the German for a few minutes, grab your rifle, and cover me from the window. Quickly, while that damned redskin is beating on the door. Posey, you stay back, stay over near the hearth." Alex yelled.

Alex drew his tomahawk from his belt and flung the door's bar aside and quickly jerked the door open. The surprised Storm Cloud stumbled through the opening attempting to regain his balance just as Alex swung his tomahawk into the intruder's neck. He struck two more times, removing Storm Cloud's head from his dying body! Alex stepped out onto the porch facing the three startled Indians. Still grasping their dead leader's head by its scalp lock, he held the dripping and bloody trophy with the shocked staring eyes up in the air and screamed defiance at the enemy warriors. Alex shook Storm Cloud's head around and then hurled it toward the three remaining warriors. The head bounced on the ground and rolled toward the frightened men.

They turned and began to run. Alex jumped from the low porch, whirling his tomahawk over his head, shifted the shaft in his hand for balance, and hurled the hatchet in the direction of the nearest fleeing Indian. The tomahawk struck the Indian and embedded itself between his shoulder blades. Before the axed Indian could fall, Billy had discharged his rifle, and the ball passed through the Indian's skull and out through his eye socket. The two remaining savages made it to their horses and attempted to escape.

Two rifle shots sounded simultaneously. Both Indians fell from their horses. Jessie and Tobias stepped from the sheltering forest, drew their belt knives, and made for the two bodies. One Indian still lived. He had suffered another gunshot wound to his other shoulder. Tobias grinned as he knelt with one knee on the young brave's chest.

"You one lucky injun. You live." Tobias noticed the two wounded shoulders. "Arms no good now for many moons. Your war days over." Tobias sliced the man's left ear from his head and dangled it in front of the brave's eyes. "I let you go. Keep ear for trophy. You tell others of this day. Not smart to attack huge white man or his friends. Go now, before I change mind and take your scalp." He jerked the brave to his feet by one of his injured arms. "No horse for you. You walk. Maybe panther or buzzards get you first. Or maybe your luck hold and you make it over the mountain, back to your people. Whichever, whatever happens to you, don't come back! Now, go!"

Billy and Posey turned their attention back now to Herman. Posey washed the wound out with water.

"Hold on, Herman, here comes the hardest part!" And Billy pressed the hot poker against the front entry wound and counted five seconds, rolled Herman over a bit, and did the same thing to the exit wound. Herman screamed. The smell of his burnt flesh was in the air.

Alex met Tobias and Jessie halfway as they crossed the courtyard. By that time the bunkhouse and barn were engulfed in flames.

"Providence brought you men back just in the nick of time." Alex grasped each one's hand in a strong handshake. "I'm not sure how this affair would have ended if you hadn't shown up and bushwhacked those last two savages. Did you see any more redskins lurking about?"

"We had been trailing them, Alex," Jessie admitted; but yesterday about noon we crossed their trail where Storm Cloud had met up with the others and headed back this way. We rode hard. The horses are worn out, probably ruined. And we didn't see anymore Indians. I think that buck whose head you removed and threw at them had bumped into these others after crossing the big mountain. That's when they decided on this raid together, that's what I suspect."

"The horses, if they're worn out, that's a small price to pay for your getting here when you did. You probably saved the day. Herman's down, he was hit at the beginning of this fray. Took an arrow in his side; Posey and Billy are cleaning him up now. I suspect he'll live."

Tobias pointed at the two burning buildings. "Too late to put the fires out."

Alex nodded. "True, our job now is to save the trading post building if we can, or at least get it emptied before the fire jumps over to it. The cabin's not in danger."

Jessie spoke up. I think that we should move as much of your stock of goods out of the building and into the cabin and onto the porch. Just in case the fire was to jump since the burning buildings are on each flank."

"I agree. Let's move the gunpowder into the cabin first, then as much of the foodstuffs as we can. The wind's coming up a bit, probably from the fire's draft." Alex led the way to the trading post building. Billy joined the three men and within a short period of time the trading post had been emptied of all their merchandise and the stored pelts.

"There she goes!" Billy pointed. The shingled roof corner nearest the barn ignited. Soon the entire structure was engulfed. All four exhausted men trudged back to the cabin and rejoined Herman and Posey. She had brought the cabin back to a semblance of order. Herman's immense bulk now rested on a bunk in the corner. Alex took the water bucket to the well and refilled it.

Upon returning to the cabin, he sat it down, turned to Posey and said, "A spot of coffee would sure set well right about now."

CHAPTER FOURTEEN

Westward Ho!

The evening was cool. Alex brought two sticks of cordwood in from the porch and tossed them on the fire in the fireplace. A hasty meal had been shared. Now Posey and the men relaxed in front of the fireplace while Herman slept on the bunk.

Jessie sipped his coffee. Poinsettia sat on the floor, knees drawn up, with her back resting against the hearth. The warmth from the fire really felt good as the shock of the day's fight and fires had worn off, leaving her feeling more tired than usual. She looked at the men. They appeared to be just as worn out as she felt. All of them were beginning to relax in the cabin's warmth. Tobias sat on the floor with his knees drawn up, his arms folded and his chin resting on his arms. He seemed to be asleep.

"You all saved our bacon today." Posey spoke softly to the four men. "That was the third time that Storm Cloud came after me. He tried just days after my parents were killed in that Indian attack on our wagon. I had seen them scalp my mother and kill my father. Mona and I were all that were left of our family. And Mona was killed by that crazy wild horse. Now this attack today. I could have lost y'all. You are all my family now. You're all that's left. And that Indian came after us again today." Posey rubbed the back of her hand across her eyes, wiping away the dampness of the almost tears.

Billy sighed. "That bunch and their misdeeds, they sure enough left us a passel of work to rebuild those buildings after we clean up what's left from the fires."

Jessie stared at the fire, took another sip of coffee, and said, "Over two years ago, I started out for Texas. Left my GTT note carved on the tree at my homestead after burning my cabin. I didn't rebuild then and I think if I build for myself again, I want it to be in Texas, on a large chunk of land open enough so that I can't be surprised by varmints anymore."

Tobias grunted. "Tobias not asleep. You all talk a lot. My people all gone too. Wife, child. No one left but you my friends. I do whatever Alex do. He wild man with that tomahawk. Like the stories told of him, he bad man with that hawk."

Alex was quiet. He thought a bit, staring into the flickering flames of the fireplace, thinking back over the day's events and those of the months and years before. "We built this place and the trading was good at first. But the settlement that the folks call Alabama Town has gotten bigger. More people came, two more merchants now are vying for the fur trade, and the Indians are on the warpath too often!" The other members of the group nodded in agreement.

"Yep," Billy agreed. And ol Jessie here, he's the first customer we've had in a spell."

Alex continued to speak. "Me personally, I don't think I want to rebuild here. I really like Jessie's idea about Texas. And, this Austin feller's offerings are sure enticing. I was thinking, if we repaired the wagon, only the wooden sides were burned, you know; but if we fixed it and bought a new tarp for it in the village, we could carry a lot of stuff at least as far, probably, as the Mississippi River. And we've the pelts still too. We could sell those to the folks at the Emporium over in 'Bama Town. Give us a bit more hard cash to carry along if we were to go to Texas."

"I'd like that sure enough. And we've enough clothing and housewares to start over. They could go in the wagon, too." Posey's voice was excited. Shyly she glanced toward Jessie and smiled.

"Our firearms are in good shape, plenty of powder, lead, and ball. And the fire didn't get into the harness bin when the barn burned, so we've all our tack still." Billy scratched his chin. "I'd like to travel on too, cause I'm just not much interested in building back here."

Jessie winked at Posey. "Be good if all of you came along. I sure wouldn't be lonesome. Be a lot safer for us...and the food would be better too, I dare say."

Herman's voice carried to the group from the far side of the room.

"If meine Freunde go to Texas, I go too!"

"Six then!" And Jessie held up six fingers.

A week after Storm Cloud's attack, the Avery party of six entered Alabama Town. While Herman was being treated by the town's doctor, they secured lodging at Ma Prentiss's boarding house. Two days later, Alex had sold the year's store of traded pelts, the group had bid Ma Prentiss farewell, and with Herman bandaged and doctored, were on the road again bound for Le Fleur's Bluff, or the newly named town of Jackson, Mississippi.

Nine days later they made camp a few miles east of the new town of Jackson, Mississippi. Three years before, Jackson, now the capital of Mississippi, had been a trading village known as Le Fleur's Bluff, for a long-ago French fur trader. Now it beckoned travelers as a bustling busy community.

Alex leaned against the wheel of their old burnt and repaired wagon and stared at the cookfire as Poinsettia worked some of their provisions into an evening meal. Billy leaned up against the opposite side of the wagon wheel.

"Alex, I think we oughta get a new wagon afore we cross into Louisiana. This one got us this far, but it's becoming a mite creaky and some of the wheel spokes are coming loose; I can turn some of them by hand in their sockets. And if that's the case, then next thing to loosen will be the iron rims on the wheels."

"We'll be in Jackson by noon or so tomorrow, Billy. Probably be a good idea to hunt up a new conveyance. Probably get one or more draft horses too, just in case one of ours gets injured. Bound to be a livery or two in a town that size. Do that, get a day's rest for Posey, and then catch the ferry across the Pearl River and head on to the Mississippi. And the Red River next, that's three good size rivers to cross."

"We need some more grain and foodstuffs, Alex. Posey said that she can see the bottom of the flour barrel and after tomorrow's breakfast, well, she said that'll be the last of the coffee."

Posey called out supper just then. Tobias supported Herman as he hobbled to the cook fire and sat down on a log that the men had pulled nearer the fire.

The six friends ate in silence, enjoying the food, and resting from the day's travel. Fifteen miles over a rough and rutted military road caused one to be bone weary. Once the campsite was squared away, they shook their blankets out and sought their bedrolls. Sleep came easy.

Not long after daylight the six companions were on the trail again. By noon they had entered Jackson. And sure enough, the new town was bustling. After securing lodging at one of the new hotels, Billy, Jessie, Tobias, and Alex left Herman and Posey in the trio of rooms that they secured. By evening time the four men had purchased a new Westward wagon that was 9 feet long as well as two new draft horses and replenished their supplies for the next leg of their journey. The following day saw the refreshed group ferry their new wagon and provisions across the Pearl River and take the road toward Petit Gulf, four days away, at the old river port on the Mississippi River. There was a ferry crossing just north of the port that would get them across the wide river to St. Jo, Louisiana.

The former Lieutenant Preston Winston Francine, accompanied by a platoon sergeant late of the U.S. Army along with a private from the 44th Regiment of Foot, a British regiment that had been attached to General Edward Pakenham's command some years before at the Battle of New Orleans, watched the group of six travelers as they disembarked from the ferryboat.

Francine muttered to the other two men. "I know two of those characters. The one with the beard, that's Billy Rudd, and the taller one on the black stallion, that's the one from South Carolina, his real name is Alexander Avery. They're both deserters. And, if you tangle with Avery, best be ready. He's quick with a tomahawk."

The short Irishman scoffed and spoke in a distinct brogue, "Looks as if they're living well for deserters. Are you certain of that fact. Lieutenant?"

"I am and they are. We're not doing anything here. Pickings have been slim lately. Let's follow them a bit on the trail, keep back out of sight though, and see where that entourage is heading....and just maybe, they might have something we can use."

The ex-sergeant in the grungy uniform jacket bobbed his head yes.

"Got a handsome looking woman with'em too. Always could be fun, give her some drink and a friendly tickle." The ex-sergeant scratched his crotch.

CHAPTER FIFTEEN

Percival O'Grady

Alex was facing west, leaning against the railing of the Merry Belle, the small steam ferry that hauled goods, passengers, and wagons across the Mississippi River from the port of Petit Gulf to St. Joseph, Louisiana on the west bank of the wide river. Alex rested his chin on his folded forearms as he continued to stare across the wide watery expanse of the Mississippi River toward the western shore and the visible roofs of the village of St. Joseph, Louisiana. It was restful, peaceful even, to view and ponder the swiftly passing water of the vast river while awaiting the completed loading of the ferryboat and its departure.

Six uneventful days had passed while he and his five companions had traveled from the Pearl River crossing to the Mississippi.

Alex continued to stare at the muddy water flowing past with the occasional snag or mass of fallen trees floating down the river. He thought of the waters crossed in the last couple of years to reach this point, "The Warrior River, the Noxabee, the Tombigbee, the Pearl, and finally, I'm seeing it, the Mississippi River. And its every bit as large and intimidating as I thought it would be. But it's the final major natural barrier to Texas and a new beginning. Now, we just have to get across the state of Louisiana and over the Red River and we'll be in Texas." Alex stood up, tall and straight, inhaled deeply, and grinned. "It has been a long haul from the Waccamaw River of South Carolina to the Mississippi, but I'm here, I and my friends!" He turned and faced the five people behind him that were immersed in the river view.

Herman sat on the wagon seat, still healing from Storm Cloud's arrow wound, and gazed across the wide expanse of water. Poinsettia had her right arm linked around Billy Rudd's left arm as they stood entranced by the massive flow of water. Billy's facial whiskers that covered the knife wound given him some years back on his face couldn't hide his smile of satisfaction. And the former stranger, now friend, Jessie Gregg stood on Posey's left side and her left arm was linked into his right arm. Tobias, always the sanguine Indian, knelt on one knee near the ferry's sideboard, watching the birds dart about the river's shallows near the Merry Belle.

"The Cherokee was always positive and confident, even optimistic at times, just like this group of wanderers." Alex thought. "In an hour or so, they would set foot in Louisiana, the last state to cross before reaching Texas."

The master of the Merry Belle pulled the whistle's lanyard two times in rapid succession, emitting two sharp blasts from the vessel's steam whistle. The group's horses corralled on the fenced-in deck behind the party's wagon snorted and flinched at the unexpected sharp sound. Two black roustabouts hauled in the gang planks from the shore's dock.

"Cast off all lines!" Bellowed the ferryboat's master. And the Merry Belle was on her way chugging across the wide Mississippi.

"Bit drier than when we crossed the Pearl River, isn't it." Posey said to no one in particular. The men on each side of her nodded yes. And it was. The Pearl had been crossed by a poled flatboat ferry making two trips each way in order to freight all the animals and their wagon. The wind had blown straight up the river with continued spray soaking their clothing. This modern small steamer was swifter and dryer even in the face of the wind sweeping across the broad river. The wind bourn waves didn't cause the vessel to rock as much either. Posey was dry, in the safe company of her friends, nay, family, and just plain happy. It was a bright day with a blue sky and puffy white clouds.

Twenty minutes later, the Merry Belle nosed up to the landing slope on the Louisiana side of the river at Saint Joseph. The roustabouts lowered the gangplanks. The standing team of horses was hitched to the wagon and Herman held the reins while Billy led the team forward slowly, easing the wagon's wheels up the sloping ramp and onto the Louisiana shore. He released the left lead horse's bridle and Herman slapped the reins against the team's backs urging them onward up the shore and to the flat gathering place overlooking the St. Joesph ferry slip. Billy returned to help the others lead their saddle mounts, the two pack horses, and the spare wagon team off the ferry.

A single blast of the Merry Belle's whistle signaled her departure from the slip. The master reversed his engine, pulling the vessel into the river's channel again, swung his ferry boat about, and headed back across the Mississippi to gather his next westward bound customers, three of which had followed Alex and Billy into the town of Petit Gulf.

Alex grinned at his friends. "Here we are, on the last of the trails across the states. Our next destination will be the promised land of Texas. Mount up, it's only noon. The sun is high in a clear sky and we're burning daylight. Lead the way west, Herman. Slap that team!" Alex trotted forward of the wagon waving his arm. "C'mon."

Jessie looked over at Poinsettia. "Think he's excited, Posey?"

"I do believe he is. And so am I." Posey spurred her mount and trotted past the lumbering wagon. Billy and Tobias rode up beside Jess.

They all laughed and kneed their mounts, coming even with Herman the German who waved with his free hand. He brushed his hair from over his ear and yelled.

"See. My brand. Slash V! Alex claimed me. I go with the group. Yee-hah! Tejas. Here comes Herman Schiller the German."

By nightfall the group had traveled 12 miles and were encamped on a long tapering hill or mound northwest of St. Joseph. Tobias had scouted the oak trees that bordered the hill below their camp. Almost silently he reappeared beside Alex near the fire.

"I am uneasy, my friend. Others have just arrived in the trees below us. There are three riders." Tobias held up three fingers. "They know we up here. They haven't made a fire. Drop blankets on the ground. Little talk, not sleep, only resting."

Alex crooked a finger at Jessie and motioned him over.

" Jess, Tobias says we aren't alone up here. Says some others have stopped in the trees below us."

Jessie looked at Tobias. "Indian or white men, Tobias?"

"White. Too quiet though. Not normal honest travelers, I think."

Alex asked, "Where exactly are they, Tobias?"

Tobias pointed in a southward direction. "Down there, almost on the same trail as us, like they were tracking wagon."

Billy noticed the group near the fire and sauntered over.

"What's going on, gents. Y'all seem serious."

Alex laid his finger over his lips and spoke softly.

"Billy, Tobias saw three white men cold camped in the oaks just south of our position on this hill. He suspects that they may be up to no good. I think that we need to take turns tonight guarding the camp. Instead of one awake and patrolling like we've done in the past, let's do it in pairs. One on each side of the camp, say south to west, the other north to east. You and Tobias take the first watch. Wake me at midnight. Jess and I will do the next one. Meanwhile, I will go and alert Posey and Herman and make sure that they keep guns by their side as they sleep. Suit you?"

"Sure, right down to the ground. Come on, Tobias. Let's get a biscuit and I need my rifle." The pair took their positions quietly, fading into the high grass and low brush of the hilltop.

Alex briefed Herman and Posey. Herman spread his blanket beneath the wagon. Posey spread hers inside the wagon beneath the seat. Alex and Jessie placed their blankets on the far side of the fire from the wagon and sought sleep before their turn at watch.

The Irishman made his way quietly to the edge of the hill's crest. He cocked his rifle, the hammer making a soft click as it locked into place. It had been so long since he had bathed that the body smell of the ex-sergeant alerted the Irishman to his presence as he crawled into a hiding place on the downwind side of him.

"Heavens above," The Irishman muttered to himself. "You are one filthy stinking man." He heard the cocking of the ex-sergeant's gun.

Preston Winston Francine stepped softly between the two prone desperados.

He spoke very quietly, almost in a soft whisper, "You two, cover me, and don't get antsy. Don't shoot until I do.'"

"Do we get to keep what we find on the bodies?" asked the Irishman.

"Don't shoot the woman. She's mine!" uttered the smelly ex-sergeant.

Francine moved around a mid-sized oak tree and came face to face with Tobias the Cherokee. Tobias grabbed the pistol that Francine was pointing toward the sleeping pair of men by the fire. Francine pulled the trigger! The hammer didn't fall. The gun failed to fire. The hammer safety had not been removed. Before Francine could shift hands to remove the safety, Tobias had a knife against his carotid artery. Francine released the pistol. The knife remained in position.

"Move toward the fire and summon your men. Do now or die!" The Cherokee's guttural command caused a prompt reaction. Francine summoned the men and told them to surrender their weapons. Compliance was immediate.

Billy came on the run, calling Alex on the way. Alex and Jessie rolled out of their blankets and joined Tobias and Billy.

Tobias grunted. "Kneel down, now! All knees on the ground." The three bandits dropped to their knees.

Alex pulled a firebrand from the campfire and held it aloft. "YOU! Damn me, it's the thieving Army Lieutenant from years ago over at Fort Hawkins in Georgia. I told you then, Lieutenant, never to let me set eyes on you again...and yet here you are. Damn!" Alex cursed and shook his head. "And who is this short stub of a man you've got with you?"

"Me name, bucko, is Percival, Percival O'Grady, late of his British Majesty's army, I am." The Irishman said. "And this smelly man beside me is Harry Osmond, he is. Claims to be a former sergeant, he does. Can we stand now, kind sir."

"No! You cannot. Stay as you are." Jessie commanded the three. "Gather their weapons, Billy, and place them in the wagon. Tobias, you said that they had horses!"

"They do. Want I should go for them?" Tobias looked questioningly at Alex.

Alex nodded affirmatively. "Bring them up here, saddles too."

Alex saw Herman coming toward them and called to him. "Herman, bring some rope."

Alex turned back to face Francine. "Just what did you have in mind to do here tonight, Lieutenant. The way this came about, looks as if you meant to rob us, or worse, kill us. That what you had in mind, you and this scum that you're traveling with?"

Francine spit in Alex's direction. "Whatever we would'a done, you had it coming. You and bushy face over there." He nodded toward Billy. "You know that you two Carolina boys were deserters, and I had you dead to rights. You know I did! Damn you!" Francine lunged to his feet and screamed. "I should'a shot you that day. I spent two months hauling waste outa the barracks and living in that pest hole of a guard house at Fort Hawkins because of you two! And without pay as well!" The former lieutenant was close enough to Alex that spittle from the berserk man sprayed Alex's face. Alex swung a hard right fist that connected with the madman's jaw and settled him face down on the ground.

"Jess, if he so much as quivers, shoot him! And you, Francine, you'd better lay still, if you value your life."

Herman came up carrying a coil of rope. "Cut some of that coil into lengths, Herman, and tie their hands behind their backs. Then get them on their feet." Alex commanded. Herman bent to his task. In moments he had pulled a loop of rope around Francine's wrists so tight that the man screamed "You're breaking my arms! Not so tight."

Herman chuckled. He cut two more rope lengths and bound the hands of O'Grady and Osmond just as tight.

Tobias led three horses into the firelight. Herman held Francine by the shoulders as the man stepped into the stirrup and swung his leg over the saddle. Billy and Alex tied Francine's legs together under the horse's belly. The same was done to the other two men.

Alex looked at the three men. "I thought of gagging you, but instead I won't. That way you can keep each other company until you find help, get scalped, or die. This is your final chance, the last time that I'll let you go, Francine. Don't come anywhere near me or my friends again, ever, and expect to live! It just won't happen again. Take heed this time and stay away!"

He gathered the three horses' reins and led them out of the clearing and pointed them north, then discharged his belt pistol into the night sky. The three spooked horses galloped off into the darkness carrying their riders, bound and helpless, screaming and cursing into the dark and vast wilderness.

Alex returned to camp. The others were standing around the fire. Alex scuffed the toe of his boot and said, "Posey, Herman, Billy, Tobias, and Jessie. I think that we should hitch the team, gather up our gear, mount up and head west at least until after daylight. Put some space between us and them, just in case they were to get lucky and somehow or with someone's aid, free their bonds and try to ambush us again."

Three quarters of an hour later they were on their way west again toward the trading post near Monroe, Louisiana. By mid-morning, Alex and his companions had traveled a good fifteen miles. They stopped, made camp, ate, and soon were asleep.

It didn't fare as well with the three scoundrels. Lieutenant Francine and his two cohorts remained mounted until daybreak. The sergeant, larger and heavier than the other two men, slid off of the saddle. He hung sideways, ending upside down on the mount. The horse bolted and drug the unfortunate sergeant into a mound of boulders. His head hit a large rock alongside the trail and burst like a melon. Percival O'Grady laughed and yelled hysterically.

"No more baths needed for you, you smelly excuse of a creature."

Finally, the horses quit running. Francine and the Irishman managed to twist in their saddles enough so that Percival was able to tug and loosen the rope that bound Francine's hands. In moments both men were free. Francine untied the bonds on the Sergeant's mount and watched coldly as the mutilated corpse dropped free.

"Good riddance. Sorry piece of stinking scum!" Francine spat in disgust.

The two men tethered their mounts, slept through the day, and into the early evening. Preston Winston Francine, former Lieutenant, U.S. Army, dreamed feverishly of the vengeance he intended to exact one day against the two former Carolinians.

CHAPTER SIXTEEN

Banks Of The Red River

Nine days later, Alex and his entourage stood on a high bluff across the Red River from the trading post built by James Coates. The trading post, built 10 years prior, now hosted a flatboat ferry that crossed the broad and deep main channel of the infamous Red River.

James Coates had recognized the natural but rare significance of the braided river system here at Bayou Pierre. The river's main channel had formed a bedload of sediment due to a massive obstruction upriver known to the local settlers as the Great Raft. The Avery party could see the numerous channels in the river's bed that had formed because of the high collection of sediment that the river's flow carried downstream. It had created massive sand bars which in turn created new and narrower channels that allowed the passage of the sediment laden waters of the river. This created varying water depths with changing current speed and strength along with a lot of quicksand bogs across the ever-changing riverbed's course.

Because of this, the Red River was a major barrier to travelers and traders attempting a southern route to Texas. For that reason the Red River was considered one of the most dangerous rivers in the world.

But now, word was that the new ferry was the solution to the crossings, and for only a 75 cents passage fee for their wagon and a dime each for every horse and rider, the ferry charge was a major bargain and improvement in the crossing of such a daunting natural barrier. Alex mounted his horse and led the way. Herman brought up the rear driving their wagon.

Alex looked over at Poinsettia as she rode up beside him and spoke to her.

"Well, Posey, its not as far to a new home place as it was."

"How far now, Alex, you reckon?"

"I'd say about six days to reach a ferry crossing on the Sabine River. I learned from the ferryman during the Red River crossing that a businessman name Taylor Gaines had established a ferry there. Seems as how it's the main crossing into a new Texas settlement known locally as Fredonia; it's located on the south bank of the Sabine."

"Do you suppose that there is any kind of inn or boarding house there, Alex?"

"Well, the ferryman said that besides the ferry, there was an office where you could register for the parcels of land given out by someone known as Haden Edwards who had the contract given a little over a year ago in 1825 by the newly formed Mexican government to bring in Anglo settlers like us. Said that for a small deposit of a couple hundred dollars a family could homestead about 4600 acres, part of it like about 170 acres for farming and the rest for cattle grazing. Billy and I had talked it over, decided that we'd both attempt getting adjoining parcels, that way we would all be working on almost 10,000 acres. Posey, I can't even imagine that much land."

Posey wiped a tear from her eye. "That caused me to remember Ma and Pa. I think that something akin to that is what they had in mind before the savages murdered them."

Alex spoke quietly. "Well, Poinsettia, its been over a dozen years since I left South Carolina to join up with the army and see the country. I'll be 30 years of age in a couple of months. I think

I'd like to stop rambling and rest a spell. I figure you must be 17 now or turning the corner on 18. Do you know? You started out across this country with your Ma and Pa and a sister. They're gone and you're still heading west. Do you ever get curious about what it might be like to homestead a place longer than three or four years?"

"Mama had taught me to read. We were gonna celebrate my being 10 years old as soon as we got down from the mountain when we were attacked. It's all getting sorta foggy now but I do remember some things."

"It does that, Posey. The better times wash out the bad."

"You know, Alex, I suspect that Jess and Billy are getting tired of the jumping about, too. Of course, Jessie hasn't been with us as long as we and ol' Tobias have been together. And now we have our friendly giant Herman with us too. I suspect that we'uns could put a place together. But my goodness! 10,000 acres! That's a big world."

"Not if you're running cattle and horses, lady. That takes a lot of grass and good water. And this land here, this east side of Texas doesn't seem too dry. Just maybe, if this Edwards man is on the up and up, we might just find out!" Alex flopped his horse's reins and increased the animal's gait. Posey followed along, grinning at the new prospect.

In five more days the Avery Party crossed the Sabine River on the Gaines Ferry and made an evening camp on the south bank of the river on a wooded knoll a mile or so from west of the river's crossing. Following the supper meal, Alex gathered them all about the campfire. Poinsettia had the coffee ready for their informal meeting.

Alex removed his hat and ruffled his hair. "Billy and I questioned the ferry operator when we crossed the Red River. This afternoon we spoke with the head honcho on the Sabine crossing. We have a pretty good idea of what lies ahead of us now. First off, it'll take us the better part of 3 days to reach the main town, the oldest town in Tejas, Nacogdoches. Both ferry operators tell us of the city's age and size. And, today, the ferryman on the Gaines Ferry said that we would need to meet with the Empresario Haden Edwards or his representative in order to acquire the land that we want for a homestead. Jimmy, wasn't it, Billy? Wasn't Jimmy the ferryman's name?"

Billy sipped his coffee and thought for a few seconds. "It was Jimmy Gaines, sure enough, and he told us that there were still some large unclaimed areas northwest of Nacogdoches. Said that as the appointed Empresario of the land grant, Edwards could issue over 800 tracts of land and that each tract would consist of 4,428 grazing acres and another 177 acres for farming to each applicant. Said that we would have to apply through him, Edwards the Empresario or one of his two commissioners; and he said that we could find one of them at the old stone fortress in Nacogdoches."

"I reckon Injun welcome too, friendly Cherokee, like me?" Tobias asked. "I'm sorta tired of rambling, always looking over my shoulder."

Herman nodded his head and brushed his hair back from his right ear, exposing the knife notches in his ear lobe. "I wear the Alex brand. I guess I get to go too, for sure."

Jessie laughed out loud. "This is sure nuff some gang of mustangs. All of us looking for a place to call home, settle down. I'd like to be counted in too. I have some coin I can contribute. And Posey, here, she's the good looking one of this bunch. She makes a good pot of coffee too, so we'd better count her in. Right, Posey?'

Posey laughed with all of them. "Sure sounds like it might take place. Have we the funds for all this, Alex? Billy?"

"Well, Posey, the ferryman wasn't exactly sure of what the Empresario's charges are, but he sure knew to the penny how much the Mexican State of Coahuila and Texas charged for each assignment of land. He told me that it was 4 cents to the acre and that the Mexican government gave you six years to pay for it if you settled on it within the first two years and began improvements to the holding."

Billy butted in. "Alex is right and I figured it up. Comes to about $ 185.00 American dollars. And if this Haden Edwards man doesn't charge too much, I think that we have enough to pay all of it outright and have some left over to buy seed and nails and such. We've got about $ 4,000.00 between us and the cattle's running wild. All you gotta do is catch 'em."

Jessie broke in. "I'll add another thousand dollars. See if you can swing two or three of those tracts. That would be enough to start a fair-sized herd of cattle, maybe some hogs too. You can get awful durn tired of just beef!"

The laughter was contagious.

Alex looked at the group. "Everyone kicks in what they can. And we all work the land, make it pay and we can have a fair to middlin' life; so if you are all agreed, say yeah!

The chorus of yeah rang out over the hill where they were camped.

Come daylight the group saddled their horses, hitched up the team to the wagon, and headed northwest toward Nacogdoches and the stone fort in search of the Empresario.

CHAPTER SEVENTEEN

Rescue

Preston Winston Francine, former Lieutenant, United States Army, accompanied by Percival O'Grady, Lance Corporal, lately of the 3rd Division, British Army commanded by Major-General Sir Edward Michael Pakenham, trudged slowly along an older trail through the pine barren.

Both men had been cashiered from their regiments, Francine for drunkenness on duty, and O'Grady for cowardice before the enemy.

Now they were embarked on a mutual enterprise; that of survival from their last foiled attempt at robbery and intimidation. Days had passed since the death of their companion and their escape from their bonds. Unfortunately for the two men, their mounts had wandered away while they slept off the effects of their ill fortuned escapade. Now they were afoot and had been for 3 days. Food had been difficult to find, not so for water. The water was brackish in the low swamp that bordered their route. The game wasn't of catchable means, and it looked as if they were going to have to eat frogs or snapping turtles raw. Neither man had matches nor the temperament and patience to create a fire by means of friction.

But thirst wasn't going to kill them, that was for sure. If one of the poisonous cottonmouth water moccasins or rattlesnakes didn't bite them they'd probably survive ....if they could find substantial food soon.

"Hey Preston, we're gonna have to stop a bit, think about some food, gentlemanly sir. This wee Irish laddie is exhausted. Hard to keep up with you, you long-legged Yank! Top of that, my front side's rubbing my backbone, it's been so long since I et!" O'Grady whined in his Irish brogue.

Preston Francine only grunted. He noticed that a break in the tree line allowed a broader view of the savannah that lay left of their path.

"Hurry up, there. Are all you Irishmen whiners. Look up ahead, we're almost out of this consarned forest and watery mess. C'mon, and hurry up. Perhaps we can find some food and transportation!"

The two men walked more rapidly and drew near the tree line's opening. They knelt in the brush and peered out across the wide savannah. The warm sunlight was inviting. Francine raised himself slightly and peered toward the northwest. There was a military encampment about 500 yards west of their position.

"Look, Irish. Look over there. That's a group of Mexican Lancers."

"The hell you say, Preston! D'ye think they might take us in, give us a wee bit of aid and food perhaps? Or stab us with them long pig stickers they're toting?"

"Both of our armies have been allies with them at one time or another in the past century. Mayhap they'll look on us with compassion if you let me do the speaking?" Francine stood.

"Stand up, Percival. Make yourself look as presentable as possible." Francine said as he straightened his shirt and tucked it into his trousers. He brushed his hair back with his hand, shot his sleeves, and made sure that his pant legs were tucked into the tops of his boots.

O'Grady did the same and attempted to stretch his length and stand straight, bracing as he had been taught in the best British military way.

"Aye, Winston, you talk. I'll only respond with yessir, and no sir. By the way, are we gonna be military vagabonds or suffering wayfarers?"

"Don't know yet, Irish. Both sound good. Let's see just how we're received and then I'll know which is the best role. You follow suit, okay!"

"Good, all sounds good! Let us go amongst them, friend Preston. This bloody Irish boy will make you and 'is mama proud of him. We're not gonna attack them or steal hosses, are we, Preston. I just want some food and a night's peaceful slumber. Aye, what say you, laddie!"

Francine looked at the short Irishman. "Just pay attention and follow my lead. And try to look like recent military, real recent."

The two desperadoes stood stiff and straight and began their march toward the Mexican cavalry encampment, waving their arms above their heads, and calling out at every other step.

There was a flurry of activity in the Mexican camp. Three mounted vedettes with lances bearing the red, white, and green pennant of Mexico wheeled their horses and galloped toward the two intruders.

"Alto! Alto!" The lead lancer was commanding the two strangers to halt.

"¿Quiénes son ustedes? ¿A dónde van?" The vedette sergeant yelled at the two men asking for identification and their intended destination.

Preston knelt on one knee. "No hablo Espanol, no hablo Espanol!" He shouted. The galloping vedettes skidded to a stop, their 8 foot long lances just inches away from Preston and Percival's chests.

The Mexican sergeant commanded the two strangers. "¡Atención!" "¡A la orden!"

The former lieutenant correctly guessed the command given by the Mexican sergeant and snapped to his best position of attention. Chin tucked, back braced, save for his filthy appearance, Francine looked every inch of the professional soldier.

Percival O'Grady did the same, even to stamping his right foot down in a perfect British Army position of attention.

Francine spoke in a commanding voice. "Sergeant, escort us to your commander!" He brushed the Mexican sergeant's lance aside and the two men marched stiffly between the mounted vedettes toward the Mexican camp. Francine spoke softly over his shoulder to O'Grady who marched in his rear.

"See the tent, the one with the national flag in front. That will be the command post, the commander's tent. Let's march directly to that. Best form now, be sharp, Irish!" And the two men marched toward the tent followed by the three mounted Mexican vedettes, lances lowered toward the two scruffy intruders.

The tent flap was brushed open by a Mexican orderly. An officer wearing a blue waistcoat adorned with red sleeve cuffs, breast collars, and gold braided epaulets stepped through the tent's opening, came to attention, and faced the two strangers and the three cavalry vedettes.

The sergeant saluted his superior officer and rendered a terse verbal report. The officer returned the sergeant's salute and evidently commanded the vedettes to raise their lances. The cavalrymen did so immediately, seating the lance butts in their saddle sockets.

The officer addressed the two strangers in English.

"Tell me who are you and how did you come to be in my country, right here, right now!"

"Sir," Francine spoke out. "Sir, I'm a former officer, a lieutenant, in the American army. My name is Preston Winston

Francine, Sir! And this sterling example of a loyal British soldier beside me. Sir, is none other than former Lance Corporal Percival O'Grady of the British Army."

O'Grady bobbed his head in agreement, stood stiff, and saluted the Mexican officer, who returned the ragamuffin's gesture out of military habit.

"Why are you two men alone in this wilderness. I see that you have no arms, your clothing is ragged and filthy, you could both use a bath, and yet you attempt to put forth a military presence. Why are you in Mexico? Speak up. I am anxious to hear this answer. Or are you spies for this group of defiant Texas colonials scattered around Nacogdoches?

"Sir, we had heard that the Mexican Government was seeking settlers for the lands above the Colorado and the Trinity Rivers, so my companion Mr. O'Grady and I put together a couple of pack horses and our own mounts about a month ago and left the state of Louisiana in search of this beacon of hope."

O'Grady was nodding his head affirmatively to Preston's narration.

Francine continued. "And sir, about ten days ago, after crossing the Sabine River down south near Green's Bluff, we headed this way. Four days past, we were attacked by some Indians. The scoundrels took everything that we owned except for our boots, pants, and shirts. They didn't even leave us our hats. They stole our horses, our packs, all of our food, our muskets, everything. We've been on foot since, trying to survive, just drinking swamp water, and eating a couple of frogs and a turtle. That's all we could catch. Sir, we're about done for. Can you spare us a bite of food, and maybe let us have a night's sleep? Some food would be awful good. Poor O'Grady's plumb shrunk up!" Francine pointed toward the Irishman.

And O'Grady moaned and rolled his eyes.

The Mexican colonel commanded his videttes. "Resume your guard duties. Go back to your original stations. Leave these men with me. Go now." He dismissed the soldiers with a courtly wave of his right arm.

"Orderly, orderly, you heard all of this. Take these men over to the soldier's mess. Get them fed. Have the surgeon check them for wounds and find them some clothing. Get them fed, doctored, and cleaned up, give them some blankets and bed them down somewhere."

The orderly saluted and motioned for Preston and Percival to follow him. Preston looked over at Percival O'Grady and winked.

"Guess we'll eat tonight!" He whispered.

Come morning, Preston stepped out of the Mexican army tent into the bright glare of the morning sun. He rubbed his stomach and yawned. "Who would have ever thought that black beans and tortillas could taste so good!" He thought to himself.

He was thirsty now. He needed water, a lot of water. As he turned to look back inside the tent, his head struck a clay botijo, or water bottle, that was suspended from the tent's support pole. It contained cool water. He drank half of the jug's contents and hung the clay botijo back on the pole. O'Grady was still asleep. Preston stepped farther into the tent and poked the Irishman in the ribs with the toe of his boot.

"Get up, you Irish sod. It's morning."

Percival O'Grady rubbed his eyes with his fists. "Were't through sleeping yet, Preston. Egads, I've never eaten so much at one time." He lifted his buttocks and farted loudly. "I need something wet, something to drink."

Preston handed him the water jug. The Irishman took a huge swig of the contents and coughed. "Ugh! That's water.

Who drinks water when they wake up. I need something stronger!"

Preston scowled at the man. "No, you need to get up and come with me. We need to find some gear, some horses and saddles. Its time for us to see about getting out of here now. And find some weapons. Shake a leg, Irish."

O'Grady splashed some water onto his face and rubbed the sleep from his eyes, adjusted his trousers, crammed his feet into his boots, and joined Preston at the tent's doorway.

The two men stepped from the tent into the bright sunlight. There was activity in the Mexican camp. A troop of lancers rode past the two men. The Colonel's orderly approached them after the last lancer had ridden past.

He nodded at the two men and beckoned for them to follow him. He led them to the Colonel's tent and held the tent flap open for Preston and Percival to pass through.

The Colonel stood behind his desk. "Good morning, good sirs."

"Good morning, Colonel. Appears to be shaping up to a nice day." Preston spoke and Percival O'Grady nodded.

The Colonel continued. "Si, it is pleasant. But we have received orders to move my command south toward the Austin Colony. I will provide you with two horses and you can accompany us or you can be free to choose your own path. Which do you prefer?"

O'Grady spoke softly to Preston. "See if we can obtain a couple of muskets and let's continue on toward Nacogdoches. Whatcha think?"

"I agree, friend Percival. I'll ask the Colonel."

Preston faced the Colonel and spoke, "Sir, we would be grateful for the loan of two mounts. By any chance, could we impose on you for the chance loan of a couple of muskets as well.

We'd like to continue on west toward the settlement at Nacogdoches. With your permission, of course, Sir."

"That country is still somewhat hostile, with Comanches and some disgruntled Americano settlers," The Colonel said. "I'll grant you a musket each and some provisions, and a horse. But, in return, I want you to carry a written message from me to the Alcade at Nacogdoches on your way west. Agreed?"

"Gladly, Sir." And Preston ducked his head yes. "Yes Sir"

"Orderly!" The Colonel barked.

The soldier entered the tent and saluted as he came to attention.

"Corporal, escort these two men to the supply tent. Have the supply sergeant outfit them with two muskets and ammunition along with saddles, blankets, and two canteens. Give them four days rations and two horses."

"Sir." The orderly acknowledged the command.

The Colonel extended his hand to Preston. "Good luck. I'll have the message prepared for you by the time you draw your gear. Dismissed."

Preston Francine and Percival O'Grady did an about face in their best military imitation and headed out of the command tent. The orderly led them to the supply section of the encampment and introduced them to the non-commissioned officer in charge. At the same time, the orderly advised the non-com of the commander's orders concerning the two strangers and then beat a hasty retreat back to the headquarters tent.

An hour later, Francine stuffed the Colonel's message to the Mexican Alcade at Nacogdoches into his saddlebags, pulled the sling tight on the 1752 Spanish musket, and mounted his horse.

He and O'Grady left the Mexican encampment at a trot and headed west.

The two men rode for several hours without stopping. They crested a small rise and pulled rein. The area in front of them was devoid of timber. Tall wavy grass lay across a wide expanse of almost a mile distant, bordered on the far side by a narrow stream bed that supported a few cottonwood trees....and two settler's wagons.

Preston tugged at O'Grady's sleeve. "We need to approach those wagons, see if we can gain an advantage, and maybe steal some clothing. We need to divest ourselves of these Mexican uniform scraps, especially the jackets."

"Why? It's a warm enough jacket." O'Grady whined. "I sorta like mine."

Francine just shook his head. "Because, Irish, if we were to bump into Comanche Indians, well, dummy, the Comanches are at war with Mexico for the most part. We probably wouldn't survive the initial meeting long enough to palaver or talk peace and trade with the Injuns if they were to recognize these uniform pants and jackets. We need more common clothes. And those settlers probably have some. So, let's ride down there and see what we can find." He spurred his horse and headed down the rise toward the grassy plain.

The black bearded man wearing the older carriage hat died first. Percival rode up behind the man and crushed his skull with a blow from the butt of his musket. Percival rode hard after a woman who ran toward the river and a nearby thicket. He caught her just before the thicket and bowled her over with his horse. Percival flung himself out of the saddle and straddled the woman. He covered her mouth to prevent her screaming and yanked off her bonnet. She was very young. It startled Percival. He jerked her to her feet and spoke loud and sharp to her. "You're coming with me. Give me your hands." He grabbed her wrists and quickly lashed them together with a thong from his saddle. Then leading his horse with one hand, he yanked the young woman along with the other hand, and they walked back toward the wagons.

At the same time, Preston charged toward a man leading two mules. The man dropped the team's lines and turned toward the wagons. Preston reined in, pointed his musket at the surprised man, and shot him. A woman appeared from behind the nearest wagon, opened her mouth and screamed. Preston slapped her across the face with his musket barrel. Unconscious, she fell to the ground. Preston dismounted, tied his horse to one of the wagon's wheels, and bent over the fallen woman.

"She ain't too young, but she'll probably be worth a horse if we find Comanches." Preston Francine muttered to himself. A short piece of rope lay beneath the wagon's seat. Preston used it to tie the woman's hands behind her and then tied the loose end to the same wagon wheel as his horse. He turned around as Percival led the younger woman and his horse over to the wagon.

"Look what I caught down by the creek, your Lordship." The Irishman grinned and snorted.

"Find yourself a piece of rope or cord in one of the wagons and tie her to the rear wheel. Then tether your horse. That way we can go through their gear in the wagons and see what we need. Might be that we want to take one of the wagons and burn the other one or at least break a couple of the wheels so that it can't be used again." Preston ordered.

By the time that Preston and Percival had plundered the wagons and thrown out the farming implements and household items from the newer wagon, the older woman had regained consciousness and was seated against the wagon wheel.

Preston approached her first and untied her rope from the wagon wheel. "Woman, we're gonna keep you and the younger woman to trade with the Comanches so you are gonna ride in the wagon and I expect you to not cause me any trouble or you'll end up like those two men. The older one, I suspect, was yours?"

"Murderer!" The woman's voice was full of malice. "That was my husband. And this woman tied to the rear wheel is my daughter-in-law! And you've killed our men. I saw you."

"We did, and you'll be next if you even make a hint at causing my pardner and me a problem. Her too." Preston nodded his head in the direction of the rear wagon wheel. He led the woman over to the rear of the wagon and lowered the tailgate. Then he untied the woman's hands. "Hold them out in front of you now." Quick as a flash, Preston looped the rope around her hands, binding them in the front.

"Now, get up into the wagon bed. Use the iron step there." He followed her up into the wagon and pushed her into a sitting position. Then he looped the rope's other end around her ankles and tied it.

Preston climbed out of the wagon, untied the younger female, escorted her to the tailgate, switched her bindings, and did the same to her as he had to her mother-in-law. With both women bound in the wagon, he climbed down and called to Percival.

"Bring that mule team over here and hitch it to the wagon. I'll tether the other wagon's horses to the rear along with your animal. You drive and I'll ride scout. Let's move on some before dark!"

The younger woman called out. "Youns gonna bury our men, my husband, and his father?"

Percival giggled. "Na, lassie, why waste time. The buzzards and the coyotes, other varmints too, I reckon, can take care of their stinking remains. You won't be here abouts to worry bout them anyways, lassie."

And with that, he slapped the reins against the mules and the wagon lurched forward.

By late afternoon Preston, Percival, and their two captives had crossed a watery bayou and halted between two small creeks a few miles south of Nacogdoches. A dusty trail led north from the nearest creek's ford. Percival O'Grady drove the wagon just beyond a small screen of young bald cypress and a few sugar berry trees.

While Percival unhitched the team, Preston dragged the two women from the wagon and propped them against the wagon until the circulation returned to their legs from being hogtied in the floor of the wagon for several hours. He grabbed the older woman roughly and shoved her toward the side of the wagon where Percival was preparing a fire pit.

"Old woman, when I untie your hands, I want you to go over there and start boiling some water for coffee and a stew. If you cause me trouble, I'll leave your carcass for the critters just like we did your menfolks." Preston untied the woman and shoved her on her way toward the fire.

He returned to the rear of the wagon, untied the younger woman's feet, pulled a bucket from the rear of the wagon, and led the woman toward the nearby creek. He grabbed her long hair and whirled her around to face him.

"Girl, your mother will need water for the cooking. Fill this bucket and carry it back over to the fire. Then you help her prepare a supper meal for us. And, just like I told her, don't mess with me or else!"

Preston watched as she filled the bucket and then carried it back toward the fire. He moved to the far side of the clearing and sat down on a log, watching the preparations.

Tobias Walking Horse eased himself from his place of concealment on the far side of the creek bank. The approaching wagon with the outrider had surprised him earlier and he had just managed to hide his horse in the brush and duck out of sight before the newcomers had crossed the creek in front of him.

He had lain there for almost an hour. Now the people on the other side of the creek seemed occupied enough for him to escape their notice while leaving the area. Tobias stealthily led his horse downstream from the newcomers' camp, mounted, and rode toward the Avery Party's camping site several miles to the northwest.

Night had fallen by the time that Tobias rode into the Avery camp and dismounted. He located Alex and spoke hastily,

"Alex, others are across that larger creek that we crossed earlier today."

"Are they following us, Tobias?"

"No, Alex, I don't think so."

"Why your concern then, my friend?"

"Alex, I recognized one of them. You would too. I think he's up to no good, Alex?" Tobias spoke softly.

"Who is it and what's the threat, Tobias?"

"It's that Army feller, the one that you threatened back after we had crossed the Mississippi River."

"What! You mean to tell me that piece of trash survived after we lashed his feet to his horse and spooked the animal!" Alex's exclamation caused Jessie and Billy to turn toward the two men. They walked over and stood with Tobias and Alex.

Billy spoke first. "Tobias, glad you're back. You brought news, did you."

"He musta." Jessie scratched his head. "He managed to wake up sleepy ole Alex here."

"Be still, you two. Let Tobias finish." Alex ordered. "Tob, where the other two, the short one and the large oafish one, were they with the Lieutenant?"

"Only the short one, the one claiming to be Irish. He with the ex-soldier. They had two women. I think they might be captives. Didn't look very happy. One woman had bruises on her face. Their clothing was torn. And they had a settler's wagon with them. If left up to me now, I'd go take the two men out, Alex. Not comfortable with them near about."

"How far from us now, Tobias?" Alex inquired.

"Not far, maybe two-hour ride if traveling quiet like."

Alex scuffed the ground with the toe of his boot and scratched his chin. He looked over at Billy.

"Billy, cuz, I want you should stay with Posey and the German. Keep the fire up and be alert. Meanwhile, Jessie and I will ride with Tobias back across the creek and see if the threat is real. If it is, well, its time to settle this once and for all!"

"Tob, get you a fast bite of vittles while Jessie and I saddle our horses and see to our gear. Then, lead us to these varmints. You said that they had a wagon. If it is as you think, that these women are prisoners, then we need to spirit them away. We could use the wagon to bring them back here."

Preparations were made and in little or no time, Alex, Jessie, and Tobias, all armed to the teeth, rode from their camp and headed down Tobias's backtrail. An hour later they descended a small rise in the land and came to a halt. About 1000 yards away, they could see the flickering firelight of the suspected enemy camp.

Alex touched his lips with his forefinger and made a motion left and right to spread out, leaving him in the center. The three frontiersmen drew a weapon each, kneed their mounts forward, and advanced quietly. They pulled up about 200 yards from the camp. They could see three forms lying beside the campfire. The fourth, one of the men, stood leaning against the wagon facing the campfire.

The trio dismounted. Alex moved over to Jessie's side.

"The one standing guard, he's staring into the fire. He'll be blind momentarily if he faces suddenly into the darkness. Wait with Tobias until I take him down, then you two come a-running. That's definitely the short Irishman. The other must be Francine. If they put up any resistance, show them no quarter. Kill them. Save the prisoners. Understood!"

Jessie nodded and moved quietly toward Tobias. Together they watched as Alex stalked the guard at the wagon.

Alex approached the wagon from the rear and moved slowly, softly feeling his way to the front of the parked wagon, stepped over the wagon's falling tongue. He lifted his tomahawk and moved within arm's reach of the short guard.

"Psst." Alex uttered the sound in a whisper. The guard turned and blinked to clear his vision. Alex recognized the Irishman. "Yell and you are dead, Irish. Where's Francine?"

"You!" The Irishman croaked. "We ain't doing nothing to you."

One of the figures by the fire stirred and set up. Alex recognized him. It was Fontaine.

"Ease your musket down, Irish, let it fall to the ground. Then put your hands behind your head. Now!"

Tobias stepped into the firelight. He pointed his rifle at the man attempting to rise. He was on one knee, reaching for the musket that was lying next to his bedroll. One of the women moved and sat up, looked at Tobias, and screamed. At the same instant, Francine lunged for his musket, swung it, and discharged the gun. The ball struck Tobias squarely between his eyes. His eyes rolled back into his head as if he was trying to see his wound. His body stiffened and swayed. Then Tobias, dead on his feet, fell backwards to the ground.

Alex wasted no time but sunk his tomahawk's blade into the Irishman's skull, hesitated a moment, and yanked it free. Blood surged from the wound. The Irishman opened his mouth like a fish gulping air and fell forward, dying without a sound.

Jessie ran toward the rising Francine. Francine whirled to meet the attacking Carolinian. Jessie slammed his rifle's buttstock into the Lieutenant's face. Francine fell hard against the ground and lay there, breathing raggedly.

Alex wiped the tomahawk's blade clean with the hem of his hunting coat and seated the weapon in his belt. He bent over and grabbed Francine's arm and jerked him into a sitting position. Jessie handed him a buckskin thong and Alex quickly lashed the semi-conscious Francine's hands behind his back. Then he grabbed the man's bound wrists and his waistbelt and jerked him to his feet.

The three men faced one another.

"Damned Deserter. You just keep turning up! I demand to be untied. Just what are you doing here. I've nothing to do with you, man!" The irate ex-Lieutenant Francine screamed at Alex. "And your companions. That damned Injun. I fixed him. Release me and I'll square with you as well!"

Alex glared at the bound desperado and spoke softly but with weighted words. "I warned you, Preston, the last time we met. I told you then to stay away from me and mine, or else be prepared to die. I meant it. And here we are again. Your partner's dead. The short Irish bugger. Now, what am I going to do with you?"

Jessie stepped over to Alex and said, "Some of the Indians back where I was raised, well, in the early days, they had a practice that worked well for some of their really bad enemies. He leaned forward and whispered to Alex.

Alex was quiet and didn't answer for a moment. He looked at Jessie and over at the two women, both who were awake by then.

"Let's check those ladies out, make sure they're okay, and then the two of us will dig a hole and do as you suggest."

Jessie nodded. The two men gagged Francine and tied him to the wagon. Then they questioned the women. The younger one blurted out that she had witnessed the killing of her husband. The older woman did the same and spoke vehemently against their captors, nodding constantly toward Francine. Alex stood up and spoke toward the women.

"Jessie and I will be working, making preparations, for a brief spell. If you two ladies can make yourselves comfortable, once we are finished here, we'll hitch the team to the wagon and take you with us to rejoin our party. There's a lady with us that will be able to assist you more if you need wounds dressed or treated. Can you fend for yourselves for a bit while we finish our preparations."

"Aye, sir. We can. And thank you for coming to our rescue. We are thankful."

Jessie and Alex found two shovels on the wagon, filled a small rawhide bag with sugar from a barrel in the wagon, and then selected a grassy spot on the creek's bank. After a deep hole was dug, they returned to the wagon, untied Francine, and led him to the prepared hole. They left his hands tied and the gag in place when they seated him on the hole's edge. Francine's eyes rounded and he attempted to yell but the gag muffled the sound.

Alex jerked the man's gag loose and drew his belt knife, leaned toward Francine, and quickly slashed both of Francine's cheeks so that a trickle of blood would roll down the man's neck. Ants would be drawn to the fresh blood, getting into the buried man's nose and mouth. Then Jessie and Alex lowered the screaming man upright into the hole. They quickly shoveled the excavated dirt into the hole, burying the standing man up to his ear lobes. They packed the dirt down firmly into the hole and added a few more spades of soil.

Alex took the small bag of sugar and sprinkled it on the filled hole around Francine's head and spoke sharply.

"I promised you that there would be hell to pay if you came at us again. So, I've sweetened the deal. This sugar oughta sweeten your meeting up with ol Scratch as you gain the entrance to hell. And the damned ants can be your escort!"

Alex and Jessie, carefully and respectfully, wrapped Tobias's body in a quilt found in one of the wagons. Then they placed his body in the better of the two wagons, hitched the team, saddled their horses, and with the younger woman handling the wagon's team, headed back toward their encampment. Francine yelled, cursed, and started crying as they rode away, leaving him behind in the darkness.

After arriving in the Avery encampment, the team was unhitched. Jessie introduced the two women to Posey, Herman, and Billy and related their loss at the hands of O'Grady and ex-Lieutenant Francine.

All turned in for a bit of rest prior to the next day's travel. Alex slept for several hours and then rose, moving quietly, so as not to disturb the others.

Untying his horse from the picket line, he slung his rifle over his shoulder and mounted. He rode out in the direction of their prior return from the camp of the two desperados.

Two hours later, just at daylight, Alex reined in about 100 yards from where they had left Francine and dismounted. Alex could clearly see the imprisoned murderer and Tobias's killer.

Alex knelt down on one knee in a shooter's braced position, unslung his rifle, and brushed the front sight clear of dust. He could see Francine's head just above the ground. Alex took careful aim and squeezed the trigger.

Francine's forehead exploded from the rifle bullet's impact. Alex stood up and slowly reloaded his rifle. When he finished with the reloading, he remounted and headed back toward his companions.

CHAPTER EIGHTEEN

Nacogdoches

Mid-afternoon two days later found the Avery party and their two wagons halting in front of the stone building in Nacogdoches bearing the sign that read 'LAND OFFICE'. Mary McCarthy and her daughter-in-law Susan joined Alex Avery, Billy Rudd, Jessie Gregg, Poinsettia Vaughn, and Herman Schiller as they entered the land office. A clerk standing behind a counter at the far end of the narrow room nodded in their direction.

"Good morning, y'all." His drawl was that of a Mississippian. "And welcome to the City of Nacogdoches. Our Mexican Government has appointed our honorable Haden Edwards as the Empresario of the land grant that contains our fair town. Do you wish to apply for land within our colony?"

Alex spoke first. "We have considered that. Myself and my adopted daughter here, Poinsettia, would like to apply for the maximum amount of land possible."

"What about the rest of you?" Asked the clerk.

"My name's Billy, Billy Rudd, and these are my partners, Jessie Gregg, and the big un, that's Herman Schiller. We'd like to apply also for a grant!"

"Mary McCarthy, that's me." The older woman spoke. "My daughter-in-law here, Susan McCarthy and I, we aren't seeking a grant, just a small house and enough land for a garden,

I think. And maybe a building suitable for a small business in town also."

Mary McCarthy had given some thought to the predicament that she and her daughter-in-law Susan was in now that their husbands had been killed by Francine and the disreputable Irishman O'Grady. Without a form of livelihood any chance of a reasonably comfortable lifestyle for them had failed to exist with the deaths of their husbands. Mary had an ace in the hole. She had been raised on a Georgia plantation and as a young girl, had fallen in love with the work in the kitchen. An elderly female slave oversaw the plantation kitchen staff and the food preparation. She had taken the young Mary under her wing sort of like a guardian angel and taught her the ins and outs of food preparation years ago. So, Mary with her knowledge of the culinary skill necessary for a restaurant continued her request to the clerk.

"I observed some of the men of Nacogdoches as we passed down the street. I had thought earlier of opening a laundry. But from my observations, I tend to think that the local townsmen would prefer good food and regular meals more than a starched and pressed shirt. So, I need a building suitable for a cafe!"

"Looks like y'all came to keep me busy for a spell this afternoon." The clerk grinned at his audience of newcomers. "So, let's get crackin' and see if we can do something here for you and our thriving community!"

And with that, the clerk adjusted his spectacles on the bridge of his nose and turned to a hand drawn map of the town that hung on the wall behind him. He studied it for a minute and turned back around to face his customers.

"Ladies first as the saying goes." The clerk sang out. "Ma'am, see right here," and he pointed toward a corner spot on the map. "This excellent corner lot faces the main street of our fair city and is open to 3rd street as a crossing point. On top of that, the lot is occupied by a frame building of less than two years old that is in good repair. The building is 40 feet wide and 70 feet long, occupying the first half of the lot. That's a 2800 square foot building. And to better the situation, there is a well on the property and a two-hole privy."

Mary McCarthy patted Susan on the back. "That sounds pretty good to us. But how much do you want for this valued property?"

"Well, the man that owned it got into a disagreement with a customer over a bet on a horse race. Our sheriff wouldn't allow the two contestants to use Main Street as the racecourse, so the race was called off. The property owner, who operated a drink and dine establishment in the building..."

Mary interrupted the clerk. "You mean a saloon, right!"

The clerk nodded. "Yes, that's what I meant to say, anyway, the property owner didn't agree with that and accused his opponent and the sheriff of collusion to defraud him. Needless to say, the Sheriff was somewhat angered and shot the building owner out of hand."

The clerk paused in his discourse and consulted some notes on his desk. He picked up one sheet of paper and waved it over his head. "Here's a list of the building's internal assets. Looks like everything is in there that you would need to start up a café immediately...and I can let you have it all, land, building, well, privy, dishes, stoves, and cooking fry pans all for one money....the low, low price of $275.00. And I'll throw in a good house cleaning for you. How's that suit you, Miss Mary?"

Susan grabbed her mother-in-law's arm. "Mama," she whispered excitedly. "There more than enough in our poke."

Following the death of O'Grady and Francine, Billy had gone through the wagon and found a poke filled with gold and silver coin hidden in a flour barrel. He had conferred with Alex and they agreed that the ladies should have the poke. After their freedom had been secured, Susan had counted the contents of the leather bag. The poke contained over $ 500.00 in gold and silver coins.

Mary nodded at Susan and turned to the clerk. "Tell you what, kind sir. I'll pay you $250.00 total for everything and the cleaning. And I'll throw in a week of free breakfasts for you beginning as soon as we can start cooking and serving. So, do we have a deal?"

The clerk grinned, scratched his ear, patted his ample stomach, and simply said "Yes"!

Then he turned to the other men. "Looks like the Nacogdoches residents are gonna start eating good cooking again soon. Now, let me see what I can do for y'all. First off, you've mentioned two land grant filings. Do you want these lands to border one another?"

Alex and Jessie nodded in the affirmative. "We'd prefer that they join somewhere. Can you arrange that?"

"Let me study the land offering map a few minutes." The clerk pulled a string down on another roller mounted on the wall and exposed a map showing an outline of the extensive land offerings.

"You'll need water access on each tract as well as plenty of grass and some timber. Hmmmm." The clerk mumbled to himself.

He pulled a map from the table and carried it from behind his counter and over to a table where Posey and the four men stood. The clerk turned the map so that the men could view it. He jabbed his finger on a spot near the upper middle of the land within a red inked border.

"These two tracts haven't been taken. They're quite a ways from here, up northwest and over toward where the Wichita River feeds off of the Red River. You're familiar with the Red River, it forms the border between Mexican Tejas and the lands of the United States of America, don'tcha know."

Alex and Jessie leaned down and peered at the map. "What's this mean here, this word 'Comanchería'. And next to it, 'Tawakonis', what's that?'

The clerk scratched his head and removed his spectacles. "Don't know much about that area. Haven't been there myself. It's in the far reaches of the leagues of land given to Empresario Edwards, there's over 200,000 acres, you know. But Tawakonis was an Indian tribe that allied with some others there abouts years past; and the Comanche, they're an Indian tribe that the buffalo hunters claim are the Lords of the Plains, a really fierce group of warrior people. All of this is some distance from the land that the United States refers to as the Indian Territories. All of this unclaimed and unsettled property is part of Tejas. That's what I know."

The clerk stood up straight and squinted at Alex and Jessie.

"But, y'all need to remember, a land league administered by Mexico is the same as that of old Spain, about two and a half miles. So a square league is equal to 4,439 acres. And two of them together, that's a big chunk of land. Those two that connect are up near the three rivers that fork off the Red, or maybe more over toward the three forks of the Trinity, or so I've been told." The clerk paused for a moment. "If I rightly recall, the buffalo hunters and scouts that have come through off and on have referred to those waters as the Upper Fork, the Middle Fork, and the Lower Fork. But I've no personal knowledge of the lay of the land. I've been told that several hundred miles west of the Upper Fork there is a gigantic canyon. I'd sure like to see that one day, don'cha know." He rubbed his head and pushed his spectacles back against his face, thought for a moment, and continued speaking.

"Now, let's see. We're charging you a nickel an acre plus an additional 3 cents an acre for administration and surveys." The clerk scratched his head. "So, that's 8 cents an acre, so your grants would be 177 acres for your kitchen garden and 4428 acres for cattle grazing, creating a total amount of land 4,605 acres. If I multiply that by 8 cents, that comes to 36840 cents and if I divide that by 100 cents, then in American dollars you'll pay me 368 dollars and 40 cents for each grant. Can you boys swing that, and you, ma'am?"

Billy turned to Jessie. "Let's step out on the porch for a minute. C'mon, Jess. You too, Herman. Alex, Posey, we'll be right back!"

Billy stepped through the door and off the porch, strode over to his horse, rummaged through his saddlebags, and withdrew a heavy rawhide pouch. He counted out 37 gold American Eagle $ 10.00 coins and put them in his hat. Do you have enough for the second grant, Jessie? And what about Herman?"

Jessie removed his hat and dropped a handful of silver and gold coins in it. "Yep. We've got him covered. The three men re-entered the room and Jessie spoke to Alex and Posey.

"Alex, you and Posey buy the first grant in your names and then Herman, Billy, and I will do the second grant jointly. I'll lend Herman the money. He's one of us now. Remember, Alex, you notched him. Let's get this wrapped up. It's been a spell since Posey's biscuits and coffee this morning. My belly's rubbing against my backbone. We need to find somewhere to eat."

Jessie slapped Herman on the back. Herman and Billy followed Jessie over to the map table and the seated clerk. They piled the coins on the table.

"Sir, there's your money. Count it out. By my calculations, we must pay you 736.80. So, there's hard coinage. Now we'd like some deeds. Do one for the McCarthy ladies' building, and a land grant deed for Alex Avery and Poinsettia Vaughn standing there, and then another one for Billy Rudd, Jessie Gregg, and Herman Schiller.

The clerk drew out three sheets of paper and an ink well and quills. "Here, then, if you McCarthy ladies will print your names on this sheet of paper, do it the way that you want them to appear on the deed for the property. And you gents, the three of you print your names on this sheet," and he handed a piece of paper over to Jessie; "and you and your daughter, sir, print your names on the last sheet. Now do print them just as you want them on the deeds. Once that's done, y'all can go find some lodging and come back tomorrow; why by then, I'll have your papers ready."

Alex looked at Billy. "I think not, kind sir. But we'll wait here while you prepare these. That's a good chunk of change on the table there, and you haven't counted it yet or made change if need be. So, we'll just hang around and watch."

The clerk seemed somewhat astounded. He started to speak and changed his mind. Instead, he nodded and went to work sorting the coins. After the counting was done, he made the necessary amount of change for each purchaser and then began the laborious process of writing up the deeds with a limited property description on each.

An hour later, the clerk leaned back in his chair, stretched his arms over his head, and stood up. He turned three completed deeds toward the buyers and pointed at the bottom lines on the papers.

"Let the two ladies go first. Mrs. Mary, you sign your name, full name, now, on the first line here, and Mrs. Susan, you sign yours on the next line down. Today is May 19, 1825. So put that date after your names. I've already signed the documents at the bottom. Once all have signed, I'll stamp the deeds with our Empresario's official seal, and we'll have all of this wrapped up."

Alex led Posey to the map table. "Okay, partner, Poinsettia my adopted daughter, sign your name where the clerk is pointing. And then I'll sign as well. Be sure and put the date there also."

Posey signed, turned, and with a big smile handed the quill to Alex.

"Thank you." She said. "Dad." And she smiled.

Then Herman, Billy, and Jessie stepped over to the table and signed their document. The clerk pulled open a drawer and retrieved a large, levered stamp and administered the seal on each document. Then he grinned a wide toothy grin.

"You five folks with the land grants, you have two years to settle and have them surveyed by Mexican law. And now, face me and raise your right hand. Do you pledge allegiance to the nation of Mexico as an honest citizen and an avowed Catholic? If so, say Aye."

All four men and Posey raised their hands, coughed, and covered their mouths when they said something akin to the word Aye.

The clerk laughed. "Just about everyone who takes that oath coughs and sputters. But it's easier here in this office than if you were to wait until the priest comes around for his next visit. Notice that no one was here to swear you in. So, the word about these parts is that we're going to start a new nation within these parts. I hear tell that Haden is planning to call it Fredonia. Haven't made it official yet though. We're waiting until Haden Edwards gets back from the United States to firm it up."

Billy stepped in front of the clerk. I believe you owe us a few dollars in change, Mister clerk. And while you're at it, I think you should make note of the fact that you've made a mistake. You see, your land grants are advertised as far east as the Mississippi for sure at being 4 cents per acre. You charged us 5 cents an acre. My calculations show that you overcharged us $ 46.05 for each land grant. That being the case, then you need to right now count us out nine of those golden eagles and two silver dollars. You can hang on to the dime for your trouble!" Billy patted the butt of one of his belt pistols. "I think right now would be a good time to conclude our business, don't you, Chubby Clerk?"

"My goodness, me oh my. How could I have made such a mistake. By all means, good sirs, and ladies, do take the maps, change, and here's the $ 92.00. With my sincere apologies, Sir."

Alex butted in. "You never said just what those Indians are known for. Are they hostile or friendly? And how many are there?"

"Sir, I honestly have no idea. I've never asked and never been told. I just know that the grants that you have are the last two parcels we have that are adjoining properties. I can only wish you well. And good day. It's quitting time now!"

Billy grinned at the clerk. "Been a pleasure making your acquaintance, Sir. But you might want to practice your ciphering a bit, just a suggestion, my friend. Be seeing you."

The seven new property owners exited the land office and clustered around the two wagons. Mary and Susan were all smiles.

"Could we go and inspect this building we bought now. I have the key. The clerk gave it to me, said that I'd need it to get inside."

"We need somewhere to spend the night. Let's pull the wagons behind the building and unharness the horses from them. We can take our mounts and the horses down to the nearest livery stable and rejoin you at your new digs." Alex pointed down the street. "That looks like the corner the clerk described if my count is right. Since this is on the corner of First Street and that's the third street down from here. Let's go see."

They unhitched the teams behind the McCarthy's building. Billy and Jessie rode down to the livery leading the two wagon teams and the other five horses. By the time that they had returned, the building's interior was being cleaned by the crew hired by the clerk at the land office. Mary McCarthy was beside herself with joy and excitement.

"They'll probably be finished in an hour or so. We've provisions and our bedrolls in the wagon. Susan, Posey, and I can fix some vittles for our supper then, and afterward, we can all bunk here inside the building. There's wood in the wood box for the stoves, and the well water is sparkling clear." She beamed at the men. "Well, what do you think. And Susan and I have decided to turn the back portion of the building into our living quarters for a year or so. Looks like the former owner was sleeping back there anyways. So, don't just stand there. Go fetch me some flour, spuds, and some beef or bacon outta the wagon. These folks will be finished soon and I'll start putting a meal together. Our first one in a new home. How perfect!"

It had been a long time on the trail since leaving Alabama. The crowing of a rooster awakened Alex just before dawn. Billy stirred in his blankets as well. Alex grumbled as he rolled over on his side.

"Damn floor's hard. Not used to sleeping in a town. Been a while. First rooster I've heard since we left our trading post. You awake, Cuz?"

Billy grunted. "Yep. Think I'll get up, find my boots, and visit the outhouse. Then take a stroll through this town just to see what's what."

Alex nodded in agreement.

The sun had been up for a couple of hours when they returned to Mary and Susan's place. Breakfast was on the table. Hungry after their stroll through the village of Nacogdoches, they joined the group at the breakfast table. Talk centered around the plans for the day. Following breakfast, Jessie and Billy went for the horses. Alex and Posey packed all of the bedrolls in their wagon.

Bidding the McCarthys good luck and farewell, Herman cracked the whip over the wagon team and the Avery group pulled out in the street. Alex rode back to the land office. The clerk was seated in a chair on the porch, sipping a cup of coffee, and watching the town come to life in the morning hours.

Alex pulled up and hailed the clerk. "Morning to you. Thought I'd tell you that we're pulling out, heading for new grants that you prepared for us yesterday. I'd like for you to send your survey team over pretty soon. Looks like we need about two or three weeks travel time to get up on the headwaters of the Sabine, then on over to where the property begins."

"I can do that, my friend. That was part of what you bought yesterday, all paid for. So it's time for us to deliver. I'll contact the head surveyor today, get it arranged. They can follow your tracks. Where you gonna locate first?

"After studying your maps, a likely place should be on the prairie nearer the Upper Fork of the Trinity River. Easiest most likely path is to point them west of the upper reach of the Sabine river over westward toward the East Fork of the Trinity; that's the first fork back this way. Cross that part of the Trinity and keep on traveling west. Use that. We'll be there waiting for them. Say about 25 days or so. That suitable to you, Clerk?"

"I'll send them on. Travel safe. The two McCarthy ladies like the building?"

"Yep. Probably in about two days, you oughta get your first free breakfast down there on the corner of Main and Third." Alex touched the brim of his hat, wheeled his horse about, and trotted up the street after the departing wagon and his mounted friends.

CHAPTER NINETEEN

Samuel Sambo

Midday, a week and one day later, they crossed the East Fork of the Trinity River. By evening time, the Avery party had made camp on the edge of an escarpment fronting a tree-filled break. The break walls were steep, but well-sloped, and covered with spruce trees and little ground foliage other than the buffalo grass. It was deceptive land. Tumbleweeds blown by the ever-present winds had collected along the edge of a grove of spruce trees. From several hundred yards away, the cluster of trees fronted by the tumbleweeds appeared to be impenetrable due to the brown wall of wind-blown thistle filled bushes.

Before darkness fell, the group had strung a picket line for their horses and built their cooking fire. Tired and weary, the group gathered around the campfire and hungrily devoured the stew that Posey had put together with some of the potatoes that they had acquired before leaving Nacogdoches more than a week before. Earlier in the day, Jessie had sat patiently on a small rise overlooking the vast plain. He had watched a small herd of antelope. Two had grazed toward him, finally coming into rifle range. He shot and dropped one of them. Its tender meat added a delicious flavor to their stew.

Alex wiped his mouth. "Well, my friends, I suspect that we're close to or on our own land now and will be for a spell.

Two leagues in each direction, plus the farm acreage, that's pushing 10,000 acres. Tomorrow let's head northwest a bit and see if we can find just where on this map from the clerk's office looks like maybe the middle fork of the Trinity River, cross it and then start looking for a suitable site to build. We need to have somewhat of a central position of both our holdings that's situated near wood and water and grassland. We can follow this break in the land that we're camped by a ways and see where it goes. That okay with y'all?"

"How long, Alex, or Dad if you prefer, do you think it will be before we can build this ranch that you have in mind? Or that all of us are thinking of?" Posey looked across the fire at Alex. "I'm about ready to have a roof and some walls around me. This constant wind blowing gets wearisome."

"Dot girl, she is richtig!" Herman the German roared out. "Do some work building us a home instead of traveling about."

Billy laughed. "Herman, you getting tired of riding that big bronc of yours. Hell, he's probably tired of you climbing on his back! Probably wishes you had a home so he didn't have to lug your huge body around! He probably wishes that you would climb back on that wagon."

"We'd probably appreciate four walls when the winter comes. I suspect that with all this wind, it probably gets a mite chilly out here on these plains." Jessie spoke softly. "I'd say, Alex, its about time we found a place and stopped, like the German says, time to do some work if we're gonna be ready for winter. Here it is the end of May. Probably only have about three months, four at the most, to get ready, Alex."

Alex nodded and yawned. "I'm in agreement with everything you all have said. Now I'm tired and sleepy. Morning will be here soon. We'll start looking for a place. It's time to go to work, as the German said."

Come morning, they were just beginning to break camp when a man was seen slowly walking toward them. Billy checked the priming in his rifle and started toward the man. Jessie headed toward the stranger as well. The newcomer didn't turn aside. He just staggered on toward them. He spoke as he neared Billy.

"Food." He said. "Food, need food." And the black man fell to one knee with his head hanging down. Hand under his arm, Jessie pulled him to his feet.

"Think you can make it over to the wagon?" Jessie asked the stranger.

"Yas suh, I can." The black man mumbled.

The trio reached the wagon. Jessie released the man's arm when he sat down.

"Posey, he's near starved I think. A biscuit and some coffee would help if there's any left." Billy said softly. "Alex, this man's worn down to a nub."

"You have a name, stranger? What are you doing out here afoot? Are you alone?" Alex watched and waited.

Between taking bites of the biscuit, the man's story began to come out. "My name, my name is Samuel, Sambo, but, but, Comanches called me Tasiwóo, Tasiwóo. Means buffalo. Like my hair. The black man rubbed his kinky hair. Months ago, stolen by Mexican slavers. Then when the slavers came into Tejas, they were ambushed by Indians. Comanches. They, the Comanches, killed all the Mexicans and most of the slaves. Didn't kill me. Don't know why. Kept me alive. Didn't get much to eat. Managed to escape, took a Comanche woman with me, she was beaten a lot by all the other women."

"Why was she beaten?" Posey asked the black man.

He finished his biscuit and took a long swallow of coffee and said, "Thank you, missus. My woman, she is half-Comanche, half Mexican. A half-breed, and younger than the others, better looking too. Think they considered her a threat to their marriages maybe. The other squaws beat her with sticks or firewood. She and I were near the river. Catching small fish for stew. The others had returned to camp. We ran away. Walked down along the stream first and then turned, waded up stream for long time to confuse any trackers. We were careful. Left no trail."

"Where's the woman?" Asked Billy.

"I left her in a hole, a hole in the wall, a cave sort of. She's weak, no food for days. I went for help. Saw you and your wagon. Thought maybe find food here." Samuel said.

"Billy," Jessie spoke up. "It might be a good idea to find her. If she's alive, and if she was of a mind to travel along with us, well, it might come in handy sometime if she speaks Comanche. I'm sure she speaks it better than what this man's acquired in his months of captivity."

"Might be. Let's mount up, get this Sambo man on a horse too; if he can ride, and he can lead us to her. Be faster than us just riding along looking for her. What do you say, Alex. That all right with you?"

"Sounds good. Herman and I will hitch up the wagon team and finish packing the camp. Then Herman, Posey, and I will head upstream and follow along on your trail. Take some jerky or something else with you for that man to nibble on. It will help him regain his strength, and her too if she's still alive when you find her. Go now. We will be along."

Two hours later Jessie pointed at the sky over a red bluff near the river. "Look at the buzzards circling."

"I recall that red rock." Sambo muttered.

Billy spurred his horse. "C'mon. Must be her whereabouts."

They splashed across the river, startling two buzzards perched on a fallen tree's limb at the edge of the creek. The vultures flapped their wings, gaining flight, and soared into the sky. The woman lay on her side under a rock overhang. She was unconscious, but still alive.

The black man knelt beside her and called her name. "Bright Star, Bright Star!"

She moaned. Her eyes fluttered. Tenderly he raised her into a sitting position and placed a canteen's spout against her lips. She drank. Then she saw the two white men and gasped; choking back a scream.

"No, no. No, be still. Bright Star, be still. You're safe now. It's me, Samuel. Drink more water." Samuel stroked her hair. "Its okay, they're friends. We have food. Here." He pressed a biscuit into her hand. "Eat, eat now. Then we'll talk. We can travel with them. Be safe from Grey Elk and the others. Eat now."

The group waited in the shade of the rocky overhang. Roughly an hour later the wagon appeared on the horizon. Jessie swung into his saddle and galloped across the creek toward the wagon. Herman pulled rein and stopped the team.

Bright Star had recovered enough to mount the wagon's tail board aided by Samuel. Posey began washing the escaped woman's wounds while Samuel sat near her at the edge of the pallet. He held the injured woman's hand and spoke softly to her, assuring her that they were safe as Posey sponged her wounds and applied ointment where necessary.

Herman slapped the reins and yelled "Giddyap, hosses, Giddyap!" And with that, the mounted men led the wagon across the stream and toward the northwest. By evening they halted at the edge of a steep bank. Below them a clear creek filled the bottom of the chasm. It couldn't be seen from a distance, only when the outriders approached the edge of the bank or cliff was it observed.

Alex rode alongside the stream for almost a mile until he found a shallow ravine leading down to the streambed. The ravine's approach created a perfect ford for the wagon and future herds of animals. Beyond the stream, on the far side, large juniper trees lined the bank all the way to the escarpment's edge. And beyond the far edge, the plains continued toward low shadowy hills in the distance. Large oaks interspersed with an occasional willow tree covered the east bank where Alex sat his horse. They extended the length of his vision.

500 yards or so, barely visible in the dim light of evening, Alex could see that the stream flowed from a rock walled pool beneath a 30 foot high waterfall.

Alex was excited. He whirled his horse around and galloped back to the others, waving his broadbrimmed hat and yelling. "This is it, this is the place. We'll build here!"

Posey stuck her head out of the canvas opening of the wagon. Alex called to her. "Posey, this is the place. You're gonna get your house with four walls. Yippee. We've found it."

That night, after supper, all of the party sat around the campfire. Samuel and the Comanche woman joined the group around the fire. More coffee was poured. The woman called Bright Star munched the last biscuit.

Alex addressed the group. "Tomorrow morning we will explore a bit, but looks like this stretch of the plains might be the perfect place for our new homestead headquarters. Best I can reckon, its about in the center of where we would want our granted lands to be. And, from what I could see before dark, there's plenty of good clear water for our use and adequate for our stock needs too. There is plenty of straight juniper trees for cabin building, oak for firewood, and the ground slopes toward the east a bit allowing good drainage. That would allow a well to the north of a privy and a barn. I figure that once we decide on the exact position for the main cabin, we should build it first. We could all sleep in it while we build a second one for us men, then give the first one to Posey and the Comanche woman. What say y'all to that?"

Billy nodded in agreement. So did Jessie, Herman, and Posey."

With that, Alex sipped his coffee and stood up. He strode over to Samuel and the Comanche woman.

"Samuel," Alex addressed the black man. "Since I don't speak Comanche and you have some knowledge now of their language, you'll need to explain to the woman what I say. And, you can begin by telling us what her name is in English, okay."

Samuel looked over at the others and spoke to Alex. "I will do that. The best that I can tell you is that her name in Comanche means Brighter Star in the Morning. So her name is Bright Star."

Then, the black man turned toward the Comanche woman and spoke her Comanche name, telling her that the whites would call her Bright Star.

She nodded that she understood and looked toward the white men and Posey gathered around the campfire and spoke in the sing song rhythm of the Comanche, telling them of her thanks for finding her, giving her water and food, and acknowledging the kindness that Posey had extended to her, and that she understood her name to them was Bright Star.

The others spoke to her almost in unison. "Welcome Bright Star."

Alex spoke again to Samuel. "I need you to understand what I am about to tell you and then for you to explain it to Bright Star. Then, after thinking over my words and our offer to you, advise me of your decisions, yours and the woman's."

Samuel nodded and quietly waited for Alex to speak.

"Samuel, you claimed that the Comanchero's had stolen you from your Mexican owners, that you were a slave, in bondage. Well, just so you'll know, we aren't slave owners. And we don't want to own anyone, much less you or the woman. As far as we, our group, are concerned, you and she, the woman, are free people, just like us.

We came here, traveling from far away to the east near the great water, the ocean, in search of a new land, a new beginning, and a place to build a ranch, a home. This looks like we've found it. This looks good, and it is part of the land granted to us, Posey, Jessie, Billy, Herman, and me from the Mexico's Empresario in Nacogdoches. So, we're gonnna build a ranch here. Anyway, if you, and Bright Star would like to join us in that effort, live here among us, and work this land with us, you are welcome to do so. Or you can leave. Stay or go. The choices are yours. So tell her and then you two give us your decision. But what ever you decide, its your own decision. You and Bright Star are free."

The black man's face registered surprise and then happiness. He turned toward the woman and spoke in halting Comanche, telling her of all that Alex had said. When he spoke of their freedom, her eyes widened, and a huge smile erupted on her face. Bright Star nodded toward the group and touched her right hand to her face and then motioned with her hand flat toward the group seated about the fire. She did this twice slowly and then begin to weep.

Posey came to Bright Star's side and rubbed her shoulder. "Welcome, Bright Star. It's good that you are here." They were friends from that moment on.

Samuel stood up and faced Alex. "I've never been free. I think that I will like it greatly. Thank you and the others for that. As you can see, Bright Star is happy too. We will accept your offer. We will work with you to build a home for all here by this stream. Thank you, Mr. Alex."

Alex looked at the others and back to Samuel. "It is good that you have decided to stay. We can do and achieve more together. And with Bright Star's speaking Comanche and your knowledge of English, Mex, and Comanche, we can talk to just about anyone who comes along. That'll sure make it easier to deal with opportunities or threats. Welcome, Samuel."

The next morning, they inspected their new surroundings, chose the best spot for the main building, and the work began. Herman, Billy, and Samuel drove the wagon to the stream's ford, found a wide suitable place on the bank near the water's edge, and turned the wagon around. Then, they began to fill it with rocks from the creek bed.

Meanwhile, Alex and Jessie laid out the foundation trench for their first building, the main cabin. The two men shoveled an 18-inch-wide level shallow trench on the rise of ground chosen by Poinsettia. It measured a full 30 feet in length with a 20-foot width.

Posey and Bright Star had turned their attention to setting up the campsite that would be used while the cabin was being built. They cleared the ground first of the prairie grass and inspected it, ensuring that there weren't any old prairie dog holes that would have afforded hidden dens or burrows for any of the ever-present rattlesnakes. Then they erected two side-walled tents and prepared a firepit for cooking and warmth, laid out the bedrolls, and closed the tent flaps.

By the time the cabin's foundation trench was completed and the campsite erected, the other three men had returned with the first wagon load of rocks. The flatter rocks were carefully placed in the trench and a rock piling support was erected at each of the four corners and one each at the center of the 30-foot runs. The three men took the wagon back to the ford for another load.

While they were gone, Alex and Jessie filled two buckets of water from the stream and dug a pit in the center of their cabin site and began to mix the water with the dirt removed earlier from the foundation trench. Then after adding a bit of short cut straw to the muddy mixture, soon, they had a reasonable amount of clay filler to place between the rocks of the foundation.

By evening, the group had completed a rock foundation for the first cabin that was 24 inches in height and its clay binder was drying hard.

The men had taken the water buckets back to the stream, washed them out, and were scrubbing up.

Herman looked at Billy. "Alex's first cabin's layout took a lotta rock, why so high off the ground?"

"Herman," Billy answered. "We all came from the East. We have an insect there that eats wood, termites, they're called. Most folks there seem to think that the termites won't climb over 18 inches in height to feast, that's the reason. And we don't know if there's termites out here on the plains or not, but why take the chance? Those rock walls will also serve as a hiding place for women and kids if there should be an attack. All that will be required is a trapdoor in the floor. That's why. Alex, Jessie, and I have built a log cabin once or twice before, I suspect."

And with that Billy splashed creek water toward the German and laughed. "You ask a lot of questions, Schiller."

"Rest your arm and back muscles well, Herman. We'll need more rock tomorrow to start laying the cabin's fireplace and chimney." Jessie grinned. "Then it'll be time to start laying logs. And that gets harder the higher the walls are. Alex has staked out a fair-sized cabin, got the work cut out for all of us."

Alex grinned at the others. "Sambo here and I just hope that the women have a lotta food cooked up. We're pretty hungry. C'mon, lets get these water buckets filled and back up to the women so they can wash up."

Come the next morning, Alex, Samuel, and Billy headed across the stream armed with three axes and a crosscut saw. It was time to harvest some of the juniper trees for logs. Jessie, Herman, and the women headed for the stream ford again to load river rock. The work progressed well throughout the day. Late in the afternoon, the men headed for the creek to bathe.

Later, around the fire, they talked and planned the next day's labor. Within an hour or so, all of them had sought their blankets and bed rolls. The noise of snoring that emanated from the men's tent could be heard across the width of the clearing.

Come daylight, the work began again. Alex explained what was needed for the logs that would form the cabin's sills.

"You only need to hew one side of the log. But measure them well. We need two prepared timbers that are fully 32 feet long, two that are 17 feet long, these two being the overlaps, and then the remaining logs that are cut won't need to be hewn on one side until we are ready for the top sills for all the walls. These will be the last logs of the structure."

"Jessie, you stay with me and the ladies. We'll mud the top of the foundation and the pillars and be ready for the first timbers that they bring to us. Also, we need to sharpen the edges on our axe blades as we will need to make drop cuts on the logs to place them on the pillars and to inter-link the logs."

Herman left the group and hitched up the team and led them toward the ford. The rest of the men carried their tools and followed along. Within an hour, Herman drove the two-horse team back across the ford dragging the first of the longer hewn logs for the sills.

Following a midday break later, the ladies dampened the top of the foundation's mud calking, and the men lifted the pre-cut and hewn logs into place, with the squared and hewn side facing up to receive the floor sleepers that would be laid crosswise the width of the building, four feet apart. They would need a total of nine hewn sleepers 19 feet 9 inches long.

"Tomorrow will require a lot of axe slinging. Arms gonna be tired, don'tcha just know it. Think we can prepare that number of floor supports in a day?" Billy asked.

Jessie grinned. "Shouldn't take all day, not with three of us slinging axes and the other two hammering the sleepers into place on the sills. That's gotta be done before we can lay the foundation for the fireplace and the chimney. Remember, boys, space has to be cut from one of the walls to mount that fireplace and chimney. That's gonna require a good bit of sawing with the correct measurements."

"Ve can do it. No problem." Herman said and flexed his biceps.

A couple of hours later, with the four sills notched and in place, the men returned to the far side of the creek where they felled a dozen more trees, topped them, and hitched them to the team, and made several trips dragging them across the stream bed to the cabin site. By then, it was nearly dark. That night, they sharpened their axes again by firelight.

When Alex rose, the morning stars were still out. He made his morning ablutions before the others were awake. After lighting a lantern, he carried it and a shovel over to the cabin site near the center of the rear wall. There he began to excavate a site for the fireplace and chimney foundations. By the time the others were up and awake and cooking breakfast, Alex had completed a sizeable foundation site on each side of the log sill and its rock foundation wall. The fireplace hearth and floor would be of stone and overlay the sill, rising above the floor when finished by 12 inches. It would extend four feet beyond the outside of the wall, allowing for the proper oversized 'scotchback' and smaller throat of the chimney to create a good draw.

Alex mused to himself. "I remember Da's first fireplace he built for his and Ma's cabin. If the wind changed direction suddenly, our home would fill with smoke; enough smoke to choke a raccoon. I was a young'un when they tore the old chimney down and built a new one with a smaller throat than the original scotchback. Won't make the same mistake that he made here on our cabin. And, I think that I'll do the entire fireplace and chimney out of rock, instead of using dobbed tree limbs on the upper chimney. Definitely will work better and last for a long time, too."

Hungry now, he headed back to the campsite to find something for breakfast. While he was working, others had stirred. Herman had gone after the two matched bays that they used for a team. They were hobbled and had grazed within a quarter mile of the camp.

Posey and Bright Star had prepared biscuits, gravy, and fatback for breakfast. The coffee was hot and bubbling. Alex eagerly asked for a plate and a biscuit. Posey plopped two biscuits on his plate and motioned toward the gravy.

"Get some, and I'll pour you a cup of coffee. Bright Star's cookin' the fatback. Alex, after breakfast, I'm going to the creek at the big hole and wash my clothes. Take a bath too, while I'm there. Keep the others away for about an hour so's I can have some privacy, please Dad."

"Take a pistol, Posey. You know how to use it if it were to be needed. Remember, strangers could be lurking around. We never know." Alex cautioned the girl.

"I'll carry that or my long knife, Dad. Who knows, I might find some berries or even a few crawdads. But just give me some privacy, okay!"

An hour or so later, Posey caught her pony and rode over to the pool beneath the watering hole. She removed her boots and pulled her bibb shirt over her head. Grabbing a bar of lye soap, she rubbed it on the spots on the shirt, then rinsed the garment out, and laid it on one of the large rocks that bordered the lower part of the pool. Then, with the soap in her hand she waded out knee deep into the pool and splashed water on her face. She knelt and ducked her head under the clear water. Coming up she started to lather her hair with the soap bar.

A breech clout and legging clad Indian warrior charged his horse out of the thicket on the far side of the pond and splashed across the yards of water between him and his prey. It all happened so fast that Posey just stood transfixed. The brave reached down from his horse, grabbed Posey under her arm, and pulled her up and across his blanketed saddle, kneed his horse around, dug his heels into the horse's flanks, and galloped out of the pool and back into the screening brush and trees on the pool's far bank.

He rode hard through the trees, kicking his horse, urging it up the steep trail to the top of the ridge. He swung right, riding hard away from the new building and the campsite. With his left arm he held the squirming Posey across the front of his blanketed saddle and rode further upriver for over a mile. He reined his horse to a skidding halt on top of a small sandy hill and unceremoniously dropped the girl from the saddle. She landed hard on her back and felt her knife sheath slam into her waist.

In a moment or less, before she could get her breath, the Indian had dismounted and landed on top of her. He shoved her legs apart and when she resisted, he grabbed a handful of her wet hair and yanked it hard. She screamed. At the same instant she remembered her belt knife. She placed her left hand against his chest, softly, and then smiled, getting his attention, and shifted her weight to her left pelvis. He eased his weight slightly, and when he did, she moved her hand into position on her knife's handle and smoothly, deftly drew it from its sheath on her belt. Just then, the redskin wrapped his hands around her throat. That's when she sank the 12-inch knife blade between his ribs beneath his heart. She twisted the knife sideways and screamed in his face.

His eyes blared, grew impossibly round, and he opened his mouth, ejecting a stream of blood, and fell to one side of her, dead. She screamed again.

"You filthy vermin-ridden beast. That's about all outa you, you, you, varmint. She stood up and brushed herself off, leaned down, and jerked her knife out of the dead hostile's chest. She cleaned the blade by plunging it into the sandy soil a couple of times and sheathed it. The Indian's horse, a black paint mare, stood where the brave had dismounted and dropped the reins.

Posey rubbed her hand over the horse's eye for a moment and then blew softly against his nostrils to quiet the animal. She took the reins, leaned against his side, and pulled herself up onto the Indian's blanketed saddle. Clucking to the horse she guided it back down the trail to the pool. She swung off the horse's back, ducked herself under the water, and washed the dead man's blood from her torso and her hair. Leading the Indian's horse, she retrieved her shirt from the large rock at the pool's edge and dressed herself. She fastened two buttons on her blouse and mounted her pony. Then gathering up the black paint's reins and leading the Indian's horse, she rode back toward their camp.

Alex and Jessie were at the stream's ford when Posey rode out of the screening juniper and oak trees on the creek's bank and splashed across the pool.

"Something's wrong, Jessie. Get your rifle!" Alex spoke sharply.

Jessie reached into the wagon and drew his long rifle out and stepped quickly to where Alex stood at the rear of the wagon.

"What did you see?" Jessie spoke softly.

"You know how modest and prim Posey is around us all of the time. She just rode down from the hillside hair uncombed and her clothing in disarray. Looked like she was wet all over, scared, and really angry! That's not like her. And she was leading a paint horse, wasn't her animal! I'm moving that way. Cover me and follow along."

Alex had advanced two hundred yards and halted. He watched as Posey neared his position. Alex called out to the girl before he stepped from behind concealment and caught her horse by its bridle. Concerned, he spoke softly to the girl.

"Posey, you look distraught. I saw you come down from the hillside. You weren't clothed when you jumped from the paint into the pool. What has happened. Are you okay right now?"

Posey dismounted and wrapped her arms around Alex. She buried her face into his shirt and began to weep.

"Dad, I just killed a man, back up on top of the ridge. Alex, it was an Indian. And he rode into the pool as I was bathing and carried me off on his horse, that one!" She pointed at the captured mustang.

"Alex, that man dropped me from his horse and attacked me. He tried to have his way with me!"

"Girl, are you hurt. Did he..?"

"No, he didn't know that I had my butcher knife or either he didn't care. He grabbed my hair, I faked him out by pretending to submit, and when he let his guard down for an instant, I stabbed him...here..." and she pointed at her heart. "He never made a sound, just bled, all over me. But I got my knife back! He's still up there, at the top of the hill. But I'm okay. I saw Indians do that to my Ma! Alex, I was scared, scared and mad. How dare someone try that, especially some man I've never seen, even met... and an Indian. Dad, he even smelled bad. Horrible, like old grease!"

Jessie had stepped alongside the pair. Alex looked over Posey's shoulder at Jessie and said, "Jess, if you'll wait here, stay out of sight, and keep watch just in case there are others about; I'll take her back to the camp and send Billy to you. Then, I want y'all to go up on the ridge, find that buck's body, and cover it with rocks. I don't want him to be found. Ever! If by chance, he is still alive, finish what Posey started with her blade. Understood!"

Jessie nodded in the affirmative. "Make haste, Alex. If he's close, send the black also. He would likely recognize any tribal markings. Might be a good idea to know where he came from."

Alex nodded, took the paint's reins and followed Posey to the campsite. Once there, he got Poinsettia a cup of coffee and a biscuit. Billy and Samuel had just returned from the far side of the stream dragging two hewn timbers. Alex called them over and explained what was needed. The two men armed themselves and rode upstream to join Jessie.

Alex checked the priming in his pistols. Then he poured himself a cup of coffee and seated himself beside Posey at the firepit. Neither spoke. Posey just took comfort in her foster father's nearness. She leaned over against his shoulder and sobbed. Alex remained quiet. He placed his arm around her shoulders.

Bright Star watched from the door of her tent. She knew something was wrong but not speaking English, she could only wonder. The woman took a cloth and dipped it into a pot of water that was warming by the fire's coals. She wrung it out and handed the wet cloth to Posey.

The girl sat up straight and took the cloth from Bright Star's outstretched hand and begin wiping her face.

"Thank you, Bright Star." Poinsettia smiled and made the sign motion from herself to the Indian woman. "Thank you."

The three men returned within a couple of hours. By this time, Posey had moved into the women's tent and was asleep. Bright Star sat in front of the tent flap until she saw the men arrive. Alex and the three men met near the new cabin. Bright

Star joined them and listened as Samuel and Jessie recounted what they had encountered.

"Alex", Jessie spoke first. "Alex, she did it right. She put that blade through his ribs right into his heart. Probably was dead before he could have grunted."

Samuel nodded. "He was Comanche, Kwahadi, the Antelope band. He came alone. I don't know why he was here in this area. He had watched us. Probably observing our movements for a day and a night at the least. He did not leave any sign of his passage, other than the remains of a small campfire, and the bones of his last meal, a rabbit. I scattered those, no trail sign now."

Jessie butted in. "Alex, he had a bow and only 4 arrows in his quiver. Had a knife in his belt. But no rifle or musket. Looks like the only horse that he had was the one that Posey rode back down the hill when she escaped. That Indian was definitely alone. I think he saw Posey as an opportunity for a captive and a quick frolic, and then after grabbing her out of the water, seeing that she was half naked, well, you know the rest."

"Y'all hid the body well enough to keep the varmints from digging him out, I guess."

Jessie and Samuel nodded. "We did. But it would be a good idea to keep our guns handy and maintain a lookout when we're working and at night for a week or so. We can rotate, take turns, you know."

"Let's get back to the others, bring them up to date. And, there's work to do. I think we need to finish that cabin! Do it quicker now." Alex led the way off the ridge and back down to the stream.

Work on the building resumed. Alex and Jessie positioned the first three floor sleepers using the exhumed fireplace foundation as the center with a sleeper in the middle of the prepared area and one each on the left and right sides of the excavation. These were fastened with pegs cut from oak branches. Then as

Herman and Billy brought more hewn sleepers from across the creek, Samuel stood the first watch, and Alex and Jessie positioned and fastened the prepped sleepers.

By evening, the foursome had returned to the wagon near the creek and filled it with the first load of rocks for the fireplace and chimney. They unhitched the team of horses near the cabin site and hobbled all of the horses so they could graze. Following supper, Herman took the next watch. Billy was to relieve him at midnight. The others sought their tents for some sleep.

Two weeks had passed since the attack on Posey. The group had worked diligently in getting the cabin finished. It stood stark against the landscape now. The chimney was built, it drew well, the floor was boarded, and the roof was laid with split shingles secured in the weight-on fashion of logs laid lengthwise on the roof. The cabin was tight. They had erected two separate sleeping quarters inside by utilizing the two tents and the wagon's canvas covering to separate one end of the cabin into two compartments.

A strong door fashioned of thick hewed planks was attached to the cabin's entrance. It was secured with the hinges that Jessie had carried from his former mountain cabin after burning it. Firing loopholes had been cut in the cabin's walls four feet apart with sliding covers securely fastened to the interior walls.

A stack of cut firewood stood on one side of the hearth and a larger stack rested outside against the cabin's front corner. The group's belongings had been moved into the cabin except for the tack, saddles, and grain for the animals. It was stored in the wagon and covered with the remaining tarp.

All was in readiness for the approach of fall and winter or a savage attack. They still maintained watches during the day and nighttime.

Plans had changed with the completion of the cabin. Alex and Jessie suggested that they build a barn for the animals next. It too would be built with logs from across the stream. Following that, a well needed to be dug near the cabin some distance above the privy. If the weather held good, a month more should see the completion of the barn and a small corral. Then, the men could turn their attention to gathering a beginning herd of cattle from the wild native longhorns that thrived in the tangled brush of the breaks.

CHAPTER TWENTY

Wounded Foot

Jessie stepped from the doorway of the cabin. He gazed across the clearing in all directions, shielding his eyes from the rising sun as he turned eastward. That's when he first saw the tendril of smoke rising above the landscape in the distance. He heard the door swing open behind him as Billy stepped outside the cabin's interior.

"You see something out there, Jess?" Billy inquired.

"Maybe." Jessie pointed to the east. "Look, against the darker hue of the sky. See that white wisp of smoke. Probably about 8 miles or more away."

"We all envy your eyesight, Jess. I don't see a thing but sky. No, wait. There it is. I can barely see it. You sure that ain't a cloud?"

Jessie shook his head no. "No cloud, too wispy. It's smoke."

Billy chuckled. "You and your far-seeing eyes. I'll go fetch us our horses and we can ride over there, see what's going on, cloud or smoke." Billy headed toward the new barn. Jessie stepped into the cabin just as Alex parted the room divider and moved toward the fireplace.

"Alex, I have seen some smoke, looks like from a good-sized campfire, some miles off to the east. Billy's saddling us a couple of horses now, we're gonna drift over that way and see who's there. It's on our lands."

"You boys be careful. Remember, we are about the only civilized people in this neck of the woods. Okay?"

"Yeah. How about that. My ma would be delighted. I'm finally civilized! Wonder if there's a couple of cold biscuits left from last night for a hungry civilized hombre." Jessie looked in the storage box on the broad wall shelf near the fireplace. "Sure nuff, here's a couple and a few slices of bacon. That'll do Billy and me until we return."

He wrapped the food in a scrap of linen hanging from the box's edge. After charging the pans of both his and Billy's long rifles, and two belt pistols each, he carried the guns and the food out of the cabin. He placed the parcel of food in his saddle bags. Jessie then hung Billy's pistol from his saddle horn and tucked a rifle into the saddle scabbard. Jessie buckled his gun belt into place and stuffed his rifle down into his saddle scabbard, then turned and strode toward the cabin.

Alex stepped through the doorway and handed Jessie two canteens filled with water then headed for the privy. By the time he returned, Billy and Jessie were riding out of the clearing toward the rising sun.

Jessie shifted his seat in the saddle slightly and moved his North pistol a bit more left so that the long frame's lock didn't press so hard against his ribs.

"Billy, with the sun up now, it's hard to see that bit of smoke. Maybe we can see more when we cross the next rise in the prairie. Gosh, it smells clean and fresh this morning."

Jessie grunted. "Wind musta not blown all night. No dust now. It does smell fresher, with a bit of moisture, you could imagine we were in the Carolina's what with the scent of the grass growing. But that'll change shortly."

"Aye, tis so. The wind never seems to lay long out here. I often miss the morning smell of the Carolina highlands, don't you."

"Yep. But you can sure see a long way off out here. Look, there's your smoke trace again. Looks like it might be coming outa that series of breaks over yonder." Jessie pointed eastward. "Tell you what, Billy, lets ride to the rim over there, dismount before we get to it, and crawl over and look down. If it were to be Indians it would be best not to be highlighted on the horizon."

That's what they did. After nearing the break's edge, they dismounted and low-crawled with their rifles to where the prairie fell away down into the rugged breaks. A wisp of pale whitish grey smoke rose from the far side of a grove of mesquite and oaks at the bottom of the broken land.

"Jessie, I don't see any Indians. Or a horse herd either."

Jessie pointed toward the left of the smoke. "Look. Is that a wagon parked beneath the trees. It's gotta be. See, it's a darker green in color than the surrounding foliage."

Billy nodded. "I see it now. Sure looks like it is. Might take us a spell to worm our way down there on foot. Be better if we can find a way down that would be easy enough to use the horses. Let's ride to the south a ways and see if we might cross a game trail that leads into the break."

They located a broken trail descending into the breaks not far from where they had dismounted. They walked their mounts slowly to keep from dislodging the scattered gravel and broken shale that littered the trail. Soon they gained the bottom and edged the horses through the tangled tree branches. Neither man spoke. They halted at the rear of the wagon in the trees. Almost 4 hours had elapsed since their departure from the ranch. A canvas tent stood between the wagon and the campfire. A man was kneeling at the fire, stirring a pan.

Jessie whispered. "Probably fixing a spot of lunch. Look, there's another man near the fire, see, the one seated sipping coffee."

The coffee drinker paused his sipping and gestured with his pipe held in the other hand. He was speaking to the one stirring food.

Billy tapped Jessie's shoulder and brought his attention to a third man who emerged from the trees pulling his suspenders into place.

Jessie made a forward motion with his hand, cocked his rifle, and together the two men stepped out of the trees behind the three men near the fire.

"Howdy. We're friendly. Can we approach the fire?" Billy called out in a stentorian voice.

The man with the pipe stood and faced the newcomers. He beckoned with his pipe. "Certainly. Come ahead on! And we bid you welcome to our humble gathering." He was polite in the extreme.

Billy and Jessie approached the fire. "I'm William Rudd and my partner is Jessie Gregg. These lands are ours. Who might you be, my friend." Billy held his rifle at port arms across his chest. So did Jessie.

The stranger with the pipe in his hand motioned toward the wagon.

Jessie glanced in that direction. Billy never took his eyes off the group around the fire.

The side of the wagon bore a sign emblazoned with the words

JAMES & MADISON-LAND SURVEYS
BEST IN THE WEST
NACOGDOCHES, TEXAS

in bright yellow and white paint. Jessie chuckled.

"Look over at the wagon, Billy, and uncock your piece." Jessie lowered the hammer on his rifle and turned to face the man with the pipe and said,

"Looks like we've been expecting y'all for a spell. You are looking for Alex Avery and Poinsettia Vaughn as well as Billy Rudd here and myself, Jessie Gregg. It's our grants that need laying out and recorded, I reckon."

The pipe holder sat his coffee on a nearby tree stump and stepped over to Billy with his right hand extended.

"Howdy there. I'm Rupert Madison. The man stirring the pan over there, that's Stephen James, my partner. The man always caught with his breeches down over there is Dennis Graham our lineman and boundary staker. And yes, we were commissioned and sent out to follow up on you boy's land grants by Haden Edward's clerk from the land office over in Nacogdoches."

Madison shook Billy's hand and extended his hand to Jessie and continued speaking. "The clerk said that I'd probably find you folks somewhere's west and north of what I call the Elm Creek Fork, off of the Trinity River. I guess that he was right cause here you are!"

The three men joined James and Graham at the fire. Jessie spoke first. "Any coffee left. We saw your smoke at daylight and rode this way. Didn't know if you were friendlies or hostiles, Indians. Thought that we'd better find out. I could sure stand a cup of coffee."

James pointed at the coffee pot seated on a fireside rock. "It's hot. There's plenty. And here's a cup. Help yourself." He looked at Billy. "Can't leave your pardner out. Here. Take this other cup and pour him some too."

Graham spoke up. "You said Indians, mister. Are there savages about?" He rubbed his head. "I hope not. I've heard of others being scalped. I'd sure like to keep my hair, Mister.

I s'pect I'd work a lot better knowing it was there!" The men laughed.

Jessie slapped Graham on the back. "We've had an encounter with an Indian or two since we left the settlements east of the Mississippi. I won't lie to you about that. But this is the frontier. And as right now, we are probably the only white folks here abouts. That being the case you might encounter some Indians. So, best be prepared for them if you do. You might have to fight to survive. One of our party, the lady named Posey, Poinsettia, encountered one, a hostile, almost a month ago. She was alone and he tried to carry her off!"

"That's not good news." Graham shuddered. "What happened to her? Did she escape?"

Billy nodded. "Yep. She did. After she put a knife through his heart!"

"Oh, my." Graham covered his mouth.

"Relax, Dennis. You'll be fine. There's three of us to do the surveying. I suspect that we'll be camped near these new friends while we do the work." Rupert looked at Billy. "We will, won't we?"

"Sure. We've been pretty busy while we waited on the surveying. We've built a cabin, and a barn as well as a corral. Now we're getting ready to dig a well. So we're pretty well fortified right now...and the only Indian we've seen during that length of time was the one that Posey knifed. And he was dead when we found him. Nothing then for us to do but bury him...and console Posey."

The party of surveyors guided by Jessie and Billy arrived at the Avery holdings not long after sundown. Alex came out of the cabin to greet them.

"I was beginning to worry a bit when you two weren't back a couple of hours ago. Who's this you've brought along with you." Alex asked.

Jessie grinned. "Remember the clerk at Nacogdoches, Alex. Well, this is the survey crew that he promised you. I'd like to introduce you to our newfound friends Rupert Madison and his partner Stephen James and their co-worker who favors his hair, Dennis Graham. They are the James & Madison Survey Company, and they are here to confirm our holdings. How about that for a morning's surprise."

"Well, a big howdy to y'all. You can pull your wagon over next to the corral and put your team up in the barn or hobble them and let them free graze, whichever you prefer. I'll go tell Posey that she and Bright Star will need to add three more plates to the meals for a spell. When you've finished setting up your camp and sleeping quarters, well, come on up to the cabin. I'll have the documents laid out and the map that we have made so that you will know how to begin your survey."

Alex went back to the cabin and retrieved his rifle and a bracc of pistols along with a canteen.

"Posey, we're low on meat with a lot of mouths to feed over the next few days. I'm going to look for a couple of antelope or deer on the far side of the ridge. I'll be back by dark."

Posey pointed the stirring spoon she was holding at Alex. "Dad, follow your own advice. Take one of the others with you. You're good, but one alone isn't safe or so you've told us." She scolded.

Alex nodded and went to find Billy.

Soon the cousins rode out and headed southwest toward the lower end of the ridge line. It didn't take long to locate a small deer herd. Two shots rang out. A half hour later, the hunters had caped and field dressed two deer, tied them behind their saddles, and were enroute back to the ranch.

They paused near a small washout and shallow stream to water their horses. The ground on each side of the stream had been heavily disturbed earlier in the day by numerous horses. All the tracks were deep indicating riders and burdens. The trail of riders led downstream in a southwest direction.

"Billy, I'd say that party numbers about a dozen, maybe a few more. And the animals aren't shod. They're Indians, looks like."

"Alex, there's probably a larger party up ahead somewhere. These riders are probably looking to join up with them. They appear to be headed just a bit east of where we shot these deer. Hope they didn't hear the gun shots. Want to follow them for a bit and see where they might be headed?"

"Its easy to see that we are outnumbered by all of these tracks. Let's skedaddle and head for home. Our folks need the meat and we need the protection of that cabin and the number of shooters on the ranch."

With that Alex spurred his horse into a lope, crossed the shallow creek, and headed home. Billy was right behind him. They kept their horses at a steady pace all the way to the ranch.

On arrival, the two deer carcasses were turned over to Samuel to finish the pot preparations and hang the meat for cooling during the night. Alex and Jessie rubbed and grained their horses. After scrubbing themselves, they entered the cabin.

Alex drew Rupert and Stephen aside and quietly told them of his and Billy's findings.

"You might want to hang around here tomorrow and maybe the next day before heading out to start your plot markings. There's no rush on our part and that would give any hostiles the time to move on out of the immediate area. Just a thought, its entirely up to you."

Rupert glanced at the floor. "Well, we appreciate your concern and consideration. I think we will follow your advice somewhat and wait until the day after tomorrow before beginning our work here. Tomorrow we can do the survey work just on this side of the stream and above it. That way we'll be within a short run toward the ranch if a problem was to arise."

Stephen agreed. The three men rejoined the others as they began to fill their plates with the steamy vittles that Posey and Bright Star had prepared.

Wounded Foot, a Comanche chief of the Tseena or Wolf Band sat on the rocky ledge overlooking the shallow arroyo that led out onto the dry plain. He was in the sixth moon of his fiftieth year and he was weary. He envied the younger warriors as they passed his resting place. Wounded Foot held his horse's braided reins and absent-mindedly twirled the leather ends through his fingers.

He thought of his tenth year of life. He was learning to care for his own horse then. Early one morning Wounded Foot attempted to gallop across the prairie hanging onto the left side of his animal with his head positioned so that he could see beneath the horse's neck. Not being physically grown, his legs were not long enough to grasp the horse's back. The horse swerved and Wounded Foot lost his balance on the horse. The horse was dragging him while he held on to the horse's neck. His feet were bouncing on the ground as he jerked about while grasping his mount's neck. Suddenly the horse's left rear foot landed on the top of Wounded Foot's left foot, crushing it. He had fallen then from his horse. It had been a long walk back to the band's camp with much pain. Wounded foot never walked normal again. Even now after all of these years, his left foot pointed far to the left when he stood or walked. His peers and the tribal elders changed his name that unforgettable day. From then on he had always been known as Wounded Foot. His thoughts drifted back to the present day.

The village's scouts had told him of the new buildings at the head of the fork of the Trinity River. And six days earlier, they had brought word of a new settlement not too far to the south that some Mexicans had fashioned from adobe. And they had already planted crops. Word among the scattered Comanche bands was that the Anglos had begun several more scattered farms to the east and that group of settlers had begun a small village in the direction of the larger settlements to the south and east.

Mexican cavalry patrols were crossing the staked plains now, following the long-established trail marked by the early iron clad and helmeted Spaniards who drove stakes into the earth to mark their route. At this rate, if what his scouts were telling him was true, soon the vast herd of buffalo that migrated each year might just quit coming into the lands of the Comanche. Then what would the people do for food...for hides for shelter....for clothing? These were nagging thoughts. Indeed, he envied the younger men as he listened to their singing and bragging of coming acts of bravery as they rode passed him. It was good to be alive, to be in on the beginning of a raid, a great raid. It had been many moons ago since he had led his warriors and those of other bands as a joint raiding party.

Wounded Foot envisioned the women that they would capture...and the children taken who could be assimilated into their tribe, the Tseena band. The last experience with the passing of the aching stomach and dripping bowel sickness had cost them many young lives. The Comanches were a family-oriented tribe. The absence of so many young boys and girls was devasting. Not to mention the lack of care that there would be later for the elderly who could literally starve to death during the cold winters on the prairie...and the reduced numbers of warriors to replace those lost in earlier battles. Yes, it was a good thing to go on a raid again. More horses, more food, maybe even some guns might be taken from these settlers. And, after a few months of becoming accustomed to the ways of the Wolf band, their young captives could begin learning the ways of a Comanche brave. It would be good to teach the ways of raiding again. He grunted happily, stood up, mounted his horse, and rejoined the cavalcade of Comanche warriors traveling southeast.

On the third day of their sojourn with the Avery group, the James & Madison Survey party had watched as Alex, Herman, Billy, and Samuel had laid out the new foundation for a bunk house.

After observing the beginning of a new building, the surveyors pointed their wagon team south and forded the stream.

The vastness of the prairie stretched ahead of them. They were familiar with their line of work and the Avery grant survey progressed rapidly. By the end of the third day of their survey, they were far advanced in the field. Then it was only a matter of swinging east on the next morning and staking and plotting the line of the southeastern side of the land grant. Then they could start the trek back to Nacogdoches and civilization that meant warm beds, reasonably good food, a change of clothes more often than a week at a time, and smooth whiskey.

Come sunup all of that changed. The surveyors had just hitched the team to the wagon, cracked the whip over the horses, and lurched out onto the prairie. Suddenly Dennis Graham pointed at the eastern horizon.

"There!" He yelled. "Look there. I do believe those three riders are Indians. Oh, my goodness!" The three riders were quickly joined by several more. They kicked their horses and rode hard toward the surveyors. Stephen James was driving. He lashed the horses. The wagon thundered across the dry land. Dennis held both his hands firmly on top of his head in an attempt to cover his hair. He never heard either of the two arrows that sank into his back. He fell off the wagon seat with his hands cupped on his head. He was dying when he hit the ground.

Two young Comanches slid to a stop by the fallen Dennis. Knife drawn, one of the men drew its edge around the fallen lineman's head and jerked the scalp from his skull and waved it toward the clouds. His victory chanting of a war cry filled the air.

Alex and Samuel saw the entire episode from a rise that they had just surmounted. They had saddled and ridden from the ranch before daybreak two days ago hoping to catch up to the surveying party. Both men were eager to make sure that the surveyors returned to the ranch before traveling back to Nacogdoches as Alex wished to discuss some further land acquisitions. Although they had proceeded cautiously, they hadn't crossed any Indian sign until they topped the small rise.

"Sambo, those men are all going to be killed unless we can stop this. Tell you what, watch your backside and follow along behind me after I've gotten their attention." Alex could see the surveyor's wagon. Two men were still aboard it but the Comanches were gaining on them.

Alex laid spurs to his horse and joined the chase. He fired his belt pistol in the air to attract attention. The Indian's gave up the chase for the wagon and turned their attention toward the two men galloping toward them.

Alex's horse responded to the sudden jerk of the bit and slid to a halt. Then Alex began to trot the animal in a circle signaling an attempt to parley, to talk. Several of the young braves started whooping again. Wounded Foot motioned for quiet, for stillness. The white man was certainly acting curiously. He motioned to one of his sub-chiefs and together they rode toward the white man who now sat still on his horse. Wounded Foot and his companion held their lances ready as they rode closer to the white man. The man held his hand out level, palm down, and swept it from his chest toward the advancing Indians.

Wounded Foot spoke from the side of his mouth to his companion. "The white man is seeking a talk. His guns are not drawn. I wish to hear what he has to say. He is either very foolish or exceedingly brave! Watch the second man, the dark one. I will speak with this white man."

Wounded Foot rode his horse close to Alex, so close that the two horses stood nose to nose. The Indian and the white man sat still, like statues, and stared at one another.

Alex held his hand out toward Wounded Foot. At the same time he shifted the fired pistol in his belt until he could withdraw it by the barrel. He extended the gun to the Indian and said, "A gift for you." He motioned to the Indian to take the gun. Wounded Foot did so and admired the pistol.

Alex again made the peace sign and motioned Samuel to come forward. Alex spoke again.

"We must be friends. Stop the attack on the men in the wagon."

Wounded Foot looked questioningly at the strange white man who was asking his dark friend to translate his words to Wounded Foot.

"Samuel, use your knowledge of their language and try to tell them as close as you can what you hear me say. Okay?" Alex never looked away from Wounded Foot. But he heard Samuel's soft reply.

"Go head on, I'm ready."

Alex pointed to himself. "I am called Alex Avery. The black man beside me is my friend Samuel. What are you called?"

Samuel spoke almost at the same time, word for word but in Comanche.

Wounded Foot listened, thought, and said, "I am called Wounded Foot, chief of the Tseena band."

Samuel translated it to Alex. "His name is Wounded Foot, chief of the Wolf band."

Alex nodded and spoke Wounded Foot's name in Comanche as Samuel had stated it. The Indian and the white man nodded at each other. Alex could see in the distance that the surveyors' wagon had halted and was loosely surrounded by mounted and waiting warlike Comanches.

Alex's next sentences were important. They could mean the life and death of all the whites. "You hunt the buffalo for food and for living. We do not chase the buffalo. We are not a threat to you or your way of life." Alex paused while Samuel spoke.

Then Alex continued. "My band, the Avery band, wishes to build a home where the river makes a pond at the waterfall. Do you know the place of which I speak?"

Wounded Foot nodded yes. "But why do you come to this place and what are these men to you?" He motioned toward the stopped surveyors' wagon.

Alex spoke again. "I and my band, we came from the mountains and the great water far, far to the east. There was unrest there. We came here to make a peaceful home. We would like to be friends. I think that we could live in peace together, you and I. But those two men in the wagon must return to us. They are part of our group, our band. I have an offer for you. Can I speak of it now?"

Samuel paused just a bit searching for the right words in Comanche to explain the great distance of travel involved.

Wounded Foot let his lance fall against his shoulder, no longer holding it in a warlike way. He lifted the pistol that Alex had given him and admired it, then turned and showed it to his companion.

He turned back to face Alex. "Speak more, through your man. His translation sounds of truth!"

Alex relaxed slightly. "My band wishes to catch the Spanish cattle, the ones with the long horns." Alex stretched his arms out wide. "We want to catch many, breed them, and create a large number, a herd of more gentle and meatier animals. You hunt the buffalo for food. We eat meat of the cattle. I offer to give to you," and Alex motioned in the way of a gift and held up two fingers.

"Two of our cows each full moon for as long as the sky is blue and the grass is tall and green. Then the people of the Wolf band won't be dependent on the buffalo if the hunt wasn't to be good. Two cows every full moon as long as our people live in peace, yours and mine. In turn, you and your band aid us by giving us protection from outsiders who aren't part of our agreement, both red and white men. Would you think that this is a good thing for all of us, your band and mine? And could we do it together, be friends and help one another?"

Alex waited while Samuel finished the translation. Wounded Foot turned to the other Indian and spoke to him, pointing to the wagon.

The Indian kicked his pony in the ribs and galloped toward the wagon.

Samuel spoke softly in Alex's direction. "Boss, he sent his companion to bring the wagon and the two surveyors over here to us, I think."

They watched as the band of Indians whooped and surrounded the wagon, riding beside it as the team was turned and pulled toward the three waiting men.

Wounded Foot held his hand out to Alex.

"You speak well, white man. Your words ring of truth. We could do this thing, be friends, your band and mine, the Wolf band. Two cows each full moon. That would be good for now. But if our band grows, or if the Tasiwoo, buffalo fails to come, would you give more?"

Alex nodded. "You and I could make that agreement. Yes. Here's my hand." And Alex offered his right hand to the Indian. Wounded Foot made the peace sign again, drew his belt knife, and with a swift motion, slashed his palm. He handed the knife to Alex.

Samuel looked at Alex. "He's offering you a blood oath. If you are in agreement and seek this friendship, slash your palm, and shake hands with him. It means that as the blood from each of your wounds mingle, you are now bound as brothers."

Alex took the offered knife and quickly slashed his palm. Then he extended his hand to Wounded Foot and handed him his knife. The two men clasped hands.

Alex nodded and said, "My Brother Wounded Foot." Samuel translated.

Wounded Foot spoke. "My Brother, Alex Avery."

And it was done.

The wagon drew up alongside. The younger warriors were all whooping. One of them yelled out in Comanche. "Why did the dead white man hold both his hands on his head. He was different, looked strange, that one?"

"Alex, they want to know why Dennis clasped his hands on top of his head."

"So tell them the truth, Sambo. He feared for his hair more than his life."

Samuel spoke quietly for the questioning Comanche warrior and the other braves. "The man you killed and scalped; he was very timid. He feared losing his hair greatly!"

The young warrior who had scalped Dennis rode back to his body and dropped the scalp on it. The other Indians were quiet now. They looked at Wounded Foot for an explanation.

Wounded Foot showed the gifted pistol and then spoke to the admiring throng. When finished, the mounted Indians waved the peace sign toward Alex and Samuel and rode off toward the horizon. Wounded Foot made the peace sign, turned his horse, and followed the departing band.

"I don't know what you did or how but you saved Stephen and me!" Rupert said to Alex. "I thought that we had bought the farm."

Stephen butted into the conversation. "Dennis was awake most of last night. Couldn't sleep. All he could think about was the possibility of getting scalped and left out on the prairie. Poor chap. Why in tarnation did that Injun take his hair back and drop it on Dennis's poor dead body instead of keeping it? What's the reasoning for that?"

Samuel looked at the surveyor. "Comanches believe that the act of scalping removes an enemy's spirit and caused them to wander between the earth and the afterlife for ever in search of their hair so that their spirit can be reclaimed. Their belief is that without their personal spirit they can never rest in the afterlife.

Because your friend Dennis held onto his hair and illustrated fear, his spirit had already fled along with his courage, so there was no honor to be gained in taking his scalp. If the warrior continued to possess it, then he would lose face and have no honor. So, he returned it to Dennis."

Samuel continued. "I was a captive of a band of Comanche. My woman, Bright Star and I escaped. These Indians are cruel and vindictive in many ways. But a lack of loyalty and no respect for truth are not in keeping with their way of life. Honor is a huge thing to them; and loss of face due to a lack of courage or even respect shown to a foe is a fearful event, talked of for many moons within their bands. I don't particularly care for their savagery or their way of life, but I must respect their faithfulness to their given word. The arrangement that the Boss here made with Wounded Foot will last long, I expect."

Samuel dismounted, walked to the wagon, rummaged around for a moment or two, and found a blanket. He carried it back to Dennis Graham's bloody corpse, broke off the arrows protruding from his back, and wrapped the man's corpse along with his scalp in the blanket. Stephen helped lift Dennis's body into the wagon bed and climbed back onto the seat beside Rupert. The party started back toward the ranch where they buried poor Dennis's corpse.

That night Rupert pulled the drawn survey maps of the Avery and Gregg grants from his leather portfolio and spread them out on the dining table where all could see the surveyors' work. Poinsettia brought another lamp over to the table.

Rupert looked around at eager faces gathered around the table.

"My friends, I think that Stephen and I should share some news with you. There is a rumor floating about in Nacogdoches concerning the affairs of Empresario Edwards and his land offerings. You see, it seems that much of the lands given to him by the newly formed Mexican Government were already held by many new settlers from the adjoining United States of America. Haden Edwards handled the claims of the newcomers verses the older settlers' holdings somewhat callously, its thought, in some circles." Rupert paused to gather his thoughts while Stephen looked at those gathered around the table and nodded in support of Rupert's words.

Rupert continued his address. "The lands that you have chosen as grants lie outside of the contested areas, thankfully. Those that are contentious in this region are only the Indians; and they of course, are not recognized as landowners by either the Mexican Government officials nor by Edwards and his appointed clerks. So, there's no one to contest your claims at this point."

Rupert looked across the table at Stephen James and continued to speak.

"After nearly losing our lives and scalps earlier today to those warlike hostile Comanches, Stephen and I discussed these issues of the Edward's grants and decided to give you all the maps that we had prepared to file. We have backdated them a month or so to the 1st day of June, 1825. And if you will note, we stretched the boundaries in the westward direction to take in an additional two leagues of land. That in all will bring your combined holdings up to around 17,000 acres. So if you keep this map that we have drawn, signed, dated, and stamped with our seal of approval, you should be protected against any encroachment from outsiders as the frontier becomes more settled. But in the meantime, your newly formed alliance with Wounded Foot's Comanche band will stand you in good stead to protect your newly formed ranch from invaders. Have you firmly decided to unite these holdings and chosen a common name? Because if you have, we can prepare a document here and now recognizing that name and joining the properties together into one holding, making it even more legal and easier to protect within the laws of Mexico and any other newly formed future government."

Alex looked around at the others as if awaiting their input. "Well!"

Jessie grinned, Herman nodded, and Billy winked at Posey. "We all asked for adjoining grants when we began," Posey smiled as she spoke, "And there's certainly no one else around to help build this place. So I think that it all needs to be owned by all five of us, that's what I think. And, I think that we should offer Samuel and Bright Star a place to live on our property for as long as they want. That's what I think!"

Alex spoke for all. "Rupert, Stephen, we all appreciate your thoughtfulness and truthfulness in these matters. Furthermore, we would like to follow your suggestion and place ownership of all of the lands, now numbering around 17,000 acres counting garden spacing, along with the water rights, in the names of us all as are accorded on the original land grants.

And as you must return to Nacogdoches two of us will accompany you for your safety against the Comanches. I think that now as we have made a pact with Wounded Foot, those who remain here will be relatively safe while we are gone. Billy and I will travel with you. That way, Samuel, who is easily recognized and speaks Comanche well, will be here with Herman, Jessie, and the ladies. Let's get some shut-eye. Tomorrow you can prepare your documents and we'll travel two days later."

Alex stood. His chair scrapped against the floor as he stood. "G'night, all. I'm bushed and need sleep."

Poinsettia stood by the fireplace as most of the others sought their beds. Billy was the last to leave. Posey walked behind his chair and brushed the back of his neck with her hand as she passed.

"Billy, there's a slice of that vinegar pie left. I'll bring it to you if you're still a mite hungry."

Billy looked up at the girl. He smiled at her. "Yeah, I could go for that. But not alone. Let's share it, you and I".

Posey's heart jumped. He had noticed her, finally. It had been days, weeks even, while they worked on the cabin and barn, while each day's grind was overcome, even when her abduction attempt had miscarried...somehow, she didn't think that he would ever notice her as a, well, as a woman. Now finally. She knew that her face must be flushed. She spoke over her shoulder as she crossed the room to prepare the pie plates.

"Billy, thank you. I would enjoy that, having pie with you. I'll be right along."

Billy turned back to studying the map on the table. "Another 8600 acres or so. Wow! That's a huge chunk of land for us to work. I wonder what old Alex has in mind," Billy thought to himself.

Posey leaned back a bit past the dividing curtain and glanced at Billy. He wasn't watching her. She took two red and white checkered cloth napkins from the shelf above the dry sink. Pulling her blouse out from her body, she stuffed the two napkins inside her blouse beneath her breasts, thus lifting them slightly and creating a fuller figure when she re-buttoned the blouse. Careful to keep her back arched and straight, she walked over to the table and handed Billy the larger of the two slices of pie.

He looked up at Posey and smiled. He thought to himself.

"Somethin' has changed. Posey looks different. Hmmm. More like a grown woman. Most color I've seen in her face for some time since that Injuns attack. Pretty girl, no doubt."

Posey flashed a smile at Billy thinking all of the time how happy she was, finally to be seen as more than just a girl. She could tell from his face that he was finally admiring her.

"Billy, can you believe it. You've been my friend and one of my constant companions for almost eight years now. I'll soon be 19 years old, I think, this year. Can you believe that. It's been so long since Mona's accident; and you, and Alex, and Jessie have been so good to me. And poor Tobias. I miss him a lot. So much has happened." Brazenly, Posey covered Billy's big hand with her small ones. "Thank you, Billy. Here, let me have your pie plate." She blushed again and hurried over to the dry sink and placed the two plates in it.

Suddenly, Billy stood beside her. He placed his hands on her shoulders, leaned forward, and kissed her on the top of her head.

"I reckon I couldn't ever hope for a better sister. I like you a lot, a whole lot." Billy spoke softly. "Think I'll get a drink of water and head for my blankets. I'm pretty tired too. Knowing this crew, tomorrow will be busy as the dickens. Best you retire now too, Posey. I'll see you in the morning. G'night, lil' Sister."

Two mornings later Alex packed some trail necessities in the surveyors' wagon. Madison and James had loaded their gear just before daybreak and hitched their team to the green wagon emblazoned with their company's name. Since Alex and Billy were serving as escorts to get the two men safely back to Nacogdoches, Alex had decided not to lead a packhorse on this trip. Instead, he planned to load his goods on the survey wagon, and once at their destination, purchase a new wagon and team for the trip back. There would be less encumbrances that way and allow for the freighting of some needed items for their new ranch.

Alex brought his big roan around to the front of the cabin and threw a blanket and saddle on him. The horse immediately blew his belly out to prevent the tightening of the saddle girth. Alex kneed him in the gut and the horse's reflex action allowed Alex to tighten the girth around the animal's belly. The horse tried to pitch a bit, kicked his hind feet, and danced about a bit. Alex dug his boot heels in and held tight to the reins until the horse settled down.

Billy was bringing his animal into view just as Alex swung up into the saddle and grasped the horn. Billy watched as the roan sunfished, trying to unseat his rider. After two more twisting bucks the big roan settled down.

The cabin door swung open suddenly. Poinsettia rushed through the door clad only in her nightgown. She ran up to Billy, flung her arms about his neck, and kissed him. Then she said hurriedly, "I love you, Billy Rudd. I love you!" And with that, she turned and ran back through the open doorway and slammed the door.

"I guess we know which of us adopted brothers Posey likes the best now, don't we. Thought she had been acting a bit strange lately." Alex chuckled, grinning as he spoke.

Billy, red in the face, said to no one in particular in a stammer, "Thought she was acting a mite strange a couple of nights ago with feeding me pie and all. But, I'm sorta fond of Posey too. If she'd said it to you or Jessie, I would'a been a mite jealous, well, sort of, I reckon."

"What in tarnation's keeping those two surveyors anyway." Alex changed the subject. "I'd like to be moving before the sun gets over the rim of the breaks."

Herman opened the cabin door. His massive bulk hid the view of the interior as he stepped out of the doorway. Jessie was right behind him.

Herman pointed at Alex. "You are well armed? Do you have plenty of ammunition?" The giant German pressed Alex's long rifle firmly into the saddle scabbard. Then he turned and checked Billy's equipment.

"I heard Posey exclaim her regards for you, Billy, my friend. Congratulations. We must make sure that you and the young woman are reunited with all of your hair in place. So pay heed, boy, to that rifle. Eh!" And Herman chuckled.

Alex grinned and said, "Herman, we're loaded for bear or whatever comes along. Just take care of the place and the ladies until our return, ok?"

"Jawohl!" Herman answered.

Jessie grinned. "The German's got it figured, Billy. Looks like Posey has chosen you as the favored one. We knew she'd been keeping an eye on you. Maybe you oughta think about finding her a ring, like, maybe a wedding ring, while you're in civilization. Surprise her sort of. We all think she's earned the right to be one of ourn. Looks like she didn't wait, since she seems to have chosen you."

Billy's face reddened even more deeply. "I, I, I hadn't ever thought 'bout marrying anyone, especially Poinsettia! Why, she's one of us, just special."

The other three men laughed. Alex pointed at Billy and spoke.

"Guess you'd best be thinking about changing your mind. Looks like we might need a white dress and some frills. And maybe something for Billy to wear besides his everyday buckskins and trousers, don'tcha just know it. And you'll need a gold ring for her as a pledge. Why in thunder don't you just climb down off that hoss and go ask her, propose a marriage now, instead of leaving here and her just wondering what you intend to do!"

Billy just stared at Alex. "Do what! I hadn't thought, you think that she would, do you? Marry me?"

Alex grunted. "You won't know, idiot, until you ask. So get down and go do it. We can wait."

Billy dismounted and rubbed his chin. "Guess I'll go see. Be right back."

He stepped onto the porch and pushed the door ajar. "Posey, can I speak to you for a moment."

"What did you forget, Mr. Rudd?"

Billy blushed and knelt on one knee, took Posey's small hand in his, and looked up at her. Stammering, he shook his head, grinned, and finally said, "You said you loved me when you ran back into the house. Well, I love you too and I want to know if you'll marry me, be my wife, when I return from this trip. They say I need a ring. I ain't got one right now, but I'll bring back a flashy one when I return if you'll just say yes! Will you marry me, Posey, will you?"

Posey thought that she would suffocate when Billy had knelt down in front of her. And then when he grabbed her hand, she stopped breathing. She took a breath again when Billy finished his question. She felt dizzy. Finally, someone to love her, really love her.

"Yes, Yes, Billy, you know that I will. Just get back. A ring's nice, but I don't have to have one. I want you, not the flash."

Billy stood up, took Posey in his arms, and covered her face with kisses. She didn't notice the wetness of the kisses or his belt gun pressing against her body. But she would never forget the moment. Her heart was filled to bursting with joy.

Billy finally let Posey go.

"I'll be back, my wife to be, I'll be back before you know it." And with those words Billy turned and rushed out of the cabin onto the porch, yelling!

"She said yes, Alex, Posey said yes!"

Billy blindly slammed into Stephen James as he and Rupert Madison finally came around from the rear of the cabin. Embarrassed by his outburst and then bumping into the two surveyors, Billy almost shouted at the two men.

"Y'all get your business done. You've shore nuff been at the privy long enough. Climb aboard your wagon and slap reins. We're burning daylight."

Alex chuckled. "Asked her, did you, Billy. Guess she musta said yes!"

"Guess you know me pretty well, Cuz.

Alex and Billy rode out first and the two surveyors followed in their wagon. Twelve days to two weeks later they likely would arrive in Nacogdoches.

CHAPTER TWENTY ONE

Ignacio

Ignacio Ruiz leaned the pitchfork against the adobe wall of the stable. He shielded his eyes against the sun and studied the mesa's rim 1200 yards to the southwest.

"Thought so. There is a man on horseback atop the mesa. He appears to be holding a lance."

Ignacio called out to his wife in their small dwelling beside the barn. "Eleana, get some water. Bring Gabriela. We must hurry and climb down into the arroyo. Hurry now. ¡Apúrate!" Ignacio retrieved a machete from a shelf inside the stable door. He tucked it into his waist sash. Grabbing a canteen of water that hung from the door post, he walked calmly around the corner of the adobe house, their jacal, to keep from arousing the lookout's suspicion.

Eleana and their daughter Gabriela joined him behind the hut. Hidden by the jacal, the family ran quickly down into the coulee . Once they reached the bottom of the gully, the trio sought refuge behind a tumble of boulders that hid a washed-out shallow cavern. Hastily, Ignacio scraped the floor of the small hiding place with the blade of his machete to run out any hiding serpents or scorpions. None appeared, so he guided his wife and daughter into the hole in the arroyo's wall and then ducked down between the boulders and his family.

The wind had risen slightly. Gusts formed dust devils that danced across the flat dry land around the Mexican jacal, stable, and corral. The blowing dust obscured the family's footprints and the remains of their passage down into the rock-strewn coulee.

The mounted band of Comanche warriors descended on the small hardscrabble farm screaming their war cries. Four scrawny chickens fled before the galloping riders. Ignacio's burro trotted to the far side of the corral. One of the braves jumped from his horse at the entrance to the small hut, shoved the crude door open, and lunged into the dark interior brandishing a tomahawk. He yelled. The jacal was empty. Two pots of food sat on a wooden table that fronted the three cots shoved against the wall.

Disgusted, the warrior dug his hand into one of the pots. The contents were warm. "Frijoles! Beans'!" The Comanche stuffed his hand filled with dripping beans into his mouth. He chewed and swallowed. He plunged his hand into the pot and filled his mouth again. Then he flung the pot across the room, kicked over the table, and exited the hut just as one of his companions shot a third arrow into the hapless burro. Two more braves were running about the dusty yard chasing the chickens.

A fifth brave thrust a burning torch into the dried grass of the hut's roof, backed his horse away from the structure as the fire caught. He shouted a war cry. He started laughing, pointing at one of the chicken-chasing Indians as he tripped and fell in the attempt to grab one of the fleeing hens. Still laughing, the Indian kneed his horse and rode to the rear of the Mexican hut. He looked across the flat land. There were no tracks in the dirt behind the jacal. He rode fifty yards toward the gully and stopped at its rim.

There was not a sign of any living creature's footprints. Nothing stirred. Puzzled, the Indian turned his horse around and trotted back to the other four braves who were mounted again and waiting near the corral.

Three of the four chickens were hanging from one of the brave's saddle, their necks wrung. The burro had sunk down to its knees, braying mournfully as it slowly died.

One Comanche asked their leader, "Shall we cut meat from the burro and take it with us on our return to the raiding party?"

"The meat is not needed. They have food. And I don't like the taste of donkey meat. It isn't as good as horse. Leave it. We can stop along the way and roast the birds that you have so bravely captured. Then we can rejoin the main party afterward." The raid's leader kicked his horse and loped toward the distant mesa.

Ignacio kept his wife and daughter in the arroyo until the shadows darkened the gully floor. Then cautiously he climbed to the rim of the coulee and lay still, watching the smoldering remains of their small holdings. Nothing was moving. The hut's roof was gone. After the burning, it had fallen into the hut's interior.

He slid back down into the gully and motioned to Elena to bring their child. When she approached, Ignacio spoke quietly to her, "Wait here with Gabriela, Elena. I will search what is left of our jacal. There might be some of our belongings remaining that we could carry with us, food, and perhaps a blanket to ward off the cold later tonight. Then we must begin our walk northeast toward the river. It is no longer safe here."

"Ignacio, I am so very tired of starting over. And the prairie, it is so horrid in its weather. And things bite. I fear for our little girl, our Gabriela. And pray that God, our Almighty God, our Father, cherishes and takes care of Gabriela....and me, and you, too, my husband," Elena looked up at her husband and brushed her hair out of her eyes. "I am sorry, Ignacio, I must not complain. I am ready now. But this time, let's hope that there is water flowing nearby and some green grass. Rebuilding then could be more pleasant...and safer. I love you, my husband, and I will follow you and help you rebuild wherever you choose."

Ignacio climbed out of the steep gully and slipped over to the jacal's ruins. Nothing remained. Ignacio shook his head in disgust and rejoined his family.

Together they followed the arroyo until it leveled out and then the three of them trudged on across the dry, flat landscape, sometimes looking over their shoulders in fear of more Indians.

CHAPTER TWENTY TWO

Cortez

Cortez Vasquez and his newest wife Fernanda were on foot. They were traveling northeasterly across the plains toward the river. Cortez led their donkey pulling a wooden wheeled cart that creaked as it moved across the dusty land. His two surviving children from his two previous marriages rode in the cart huddled under some hay that provided a measure of warmth against the nighttime chill. Unknown to Cortez, only eight miles separated him from Ignacio and his family who were also fleeing across the prairie. Both families had survived attacks from the larger Comanche raiding party. But the Vasquez family had not fared as well as the Ruiz family.

The Comanches had attacked just at dusk. There had been no warning. The Vasquez's yard dog had been lanced quickly by the Indians before it could bark a warning. When a trio of Indians had burst into the family's dwelling, Cortez had killed the three invaders with his machete. Cortez, a large framed bear of a man had not been quick enough to prevent two of his older boys from rushing out of the house. His two sons were killed immediately. Their scalps now adorned the lances of two of the raiders.

Meanwhile, Cortez, his wife, along with their surviving son and daughter had sought safety beneath the floor of their home. A trapdoor in the floor concealed by a cleverly attached wool rug provided a rapid escape for the beleaguered family. The hidden cellar had a short tunnel that led into a nearby ravine.

The attacking Comanches fired the Cortez home. They killed the two milk cows in the ramshackle thatched roof structure serving as a cowshed, lanced three pigs, a sow and two piglets, and scalped the two fallen Mexican boys. Then, waving the scalps and with the piglet carcasses thrown over their saddles, and yelling their war cries, the remaining raiders galloped away from the burning Mexican homestead.

Darkness concealed Cortez, Fernanda, and the two younger children in their escape from the cellar. But they had no water or food, only the clothes that they wore as they began their trek to the northeast and maybe safety. Their donkey had been overlooked as had the cart standing near their corral. At least something had remained of their former homestead. But the two elder sons were dead. Cortez's heart was heavy. He thought of his former wives, one dead from cholera and Topaz, the second wife, only a year later lost to yellow fever. Now, their sons were dead too. But Cortez wasn't a quitter.

"Merciful Father. Please to give me courage. Blessed Virgin, remember my wife and children. Father, smooth the way for my sons into your Heaven." He thought to himself. He made the sign of the cross and walked on. That's when he saw people coming toward him and his new wife.

"Look, Fernanda, there's three people moving toward us. You can see them. They are illuminated by the sunrise. Look, see them there!" Cortez pointed northward.

"I see them, Cortez. They do not appear to be ferocious Indians. Perhaps they have some water. Let's move toward them." Fernanda said excitedly. She began to wave her arms over her head. The two small children, a boy and a girl, did the same.

Overjoyed, Fernanda spoke to her husband and pointed in the direction of the couple walking toward them, "Look, they are waving at us too. Wave back, Cortez, wave at them so they will know we are not hostiles!"

Alex and Billy were in Nacogdoches for only a day. They had successfully recorded their holdings, procured the group's needed supplies along with an engagement ring, and a wedding dress. They checked on the well-being of the McCarthy women and enjoyed a sit-down meal at their now bustling café. Come sunrise, Billy urged their new wagon's team into the bustling main street. His riding horse was tethered to the wagon's rear. Alex mounted and rode out of town slightly ahead of the wagon. The prairie stretched off into the distance ahead of them. By nightfall they had uneventfully traveled about 20 miles toward home. The new team's horses were strong and well matched. Billy was frying fatback for their evening meal. The coffee was ready. Alex drug a nearby log over to the fire for his and Billy's seating. He straightened quickly, drew his pistol from his belt, and motioned to the north, saying,

"Cuz, be alert. There's someone or some people moving toward us. I hear them, can't see them yet, but they're coming this way. Sounds as if they've got a conveyance, too. I just heard its wheels creak."

Billy sat the frying pan down and moved to the wagon. He withdrew his rifle from beneath the seat, stepped down from the wagon's wheel, and shouldered the gun and cocked it just as a disheveled couple led a donkey and its cart into the firelight.

"Hold and stand still!" Billy shouted from the wagon's concealment.

"Don't shoot, Americano, we are seeking refuge, my Mexicano companions and me. Mi nombre es Cortez. Cortez Vasquez is my name, and with me is my wife Fernanda, and our two children are in the donkey cart. And my new friends, Ignacio and

Elena Ruiz, and their small daughter Gabriela. We seek safety, some food and water. The Comanches burned our homes and drove us away from our farms. In the name of the Virgin Mother, can you help us, por favor."

Alex called to Billy. "Cover them, Cuz. But hold your fire. I'll check them out."

Alex sprinted past the group of Mexicans with his pistol drawn and checked their back trail. He returned to the group quickly and checked the cart for weapons.

"It appears to be safe, Billy. There are only two machetes among them and the men are armed with those. As he said, there's only two women and three kids."

Billy stepped from behind the wagon, his rifle cradled in his arm. He walked over to Cortez. "Are any of you wounded or hurt?"

Cortez spoke quickly. "No, senor, no one is hurt. But the women, and the children, they have much thirst. We've had no water since early this morning. There was only one canteen. It was carried by the Ruiz family and it was only half full. Not much for seven people on this hot day. We, my wife and I, and Ignacio and his wife and child, along with my two children, got away from the Comanches yesterday evening. We've walked since then hoping to not be found by the hostiles. We must seek a new place to grow food and build our homes now. Have you any food that you can share? The children, they are hungry, senor."

"Senor Cortez, we can feed your people. Park your cart over behind yon wagon and hobble your donkey so he can graze. You can draw water from the water barrel on our wagon for your animal and your families.

Meanwhile, I'll scare up some grub, food, for us and your people. Get everyone fed and watered down, then we'll talk. Okay?"

"Muchas gracias, señor, muchas gracias."

Alex watched as the two Mexican men drew water from the wagon's water barrel. Ignacio and Cortez gave the three children water first. Then they drew water for their wives, and finally after their families had quenched their thirst, the two men drank their fill.

Billy unpacked more food from their supplies. He fried more fatback, prepared a pot of beans, and a dutch oven full of biscuits. Elena and Fernanda were given blankets to make a pallet for the children in the donkey cart. Soon the food was cooked and eaten. The children were asleep in the cart, and the six adults sat around the fire, sipping coffee.

Billy nodded to Cortez. "Does Ignacio speak English."

Ignacio stood up. "Si, Señor. I speak some, but not always so good. But Cortez, it seems he speaks the english well. I will listen to the two of you talk, and then we can inform our wives. Then they can answer and we can tell you what it is they say, okay?"

An hour passed rapidly with the telling of the attacks and the journeys across the plains. Billy and Alex listened intently. After Cortez had finished the telling of their disasters and fears of the Comanche as well as their needing new home sites, Billy scratched his head.

"Alex, these folks are gonna need a place to begin again, to start new lives. Sorta like what happened to us back in Alabama, you know. But, I've been thinking some while the Mexican fellers have been speaking. We're gonna attempt to build a big spread or ranch. You've been hankering to start gathering wild cows, these longhorns that seem to be hiding in all the arroyos and breaks out here. Well, if we do that, we're going to need some more hands, herders, some riders to do this. We can't do all the building, and all cattle searching with just the five of us men."

"What are you building up too, Billy. You're getting a bit long-winded." Alex leaned over and poured more coffee into his cup.

"Alright, straight to it, Alex. I don't have qualms or aversions to having them settle on the ranch we're building and come to work for us. They could erect their own dwellings and do some farming too. And, we've laid the foundation for the new bunkhouse next to the barn. We could sure use some more help in building that. If we all worked together, we'd probably eat better, live better, and with seven men and four womenfolk, we could make something great outa that chunk of land. It has plenty of water, timber, and grassland, more than enough to go around. And, I suspect that we could have the buildings finished and chinked before winter sets in."

"Billy, that's pretty good thinking. I like it. Let's tell the men. See if they might be interested. One thing, though."

"What's that, Alex?" Billy squinted at his cousin when he spoke.

"If they agree, we'll need to turn around, go back to the settlement, and buy some more supplies. We don't have enough staples like flour and so forth, not for this many people. That will eat into our savings a bit more." He paused. "And add at least two more days to our journey, take us longer to arrive back at the homesteads.

Billy nodded in agreement. "Yes but think about what it will mean later. And, I think we can afford the extra. Probably need to warn the townspeople about these damned Comanche raiders too. Just as you say, that will put us at least two or three days later in getting home. You reckon Jess and Posey and the others will be safe until we get back?"

Alex rubbed his chin and stared at the fire for a moment. "Well, we made good time today. I see no reason that we can't double back and be quick about it. The horses are reasonably fresh. If we don't take the wagon, maybe leave it here and only one of us go...I think we can gain a day. Yeah, I think they'll be okay."

The two cousins called Cortez and Ignacio over to the fire.

"Cortez, Ignacio," Billy said. "My cousin here, Alex, well, he and I are partners in a ranch that we are building on Elm Creek Fork of the Trinity River, that's at least nine or ten long days journey northwest of here by wagon."

The two Mexicans nodded.

Billy continued to speak. "We plan to create a herd of cattle by catching these wild Texas longhorns, gentle them down some, fatten them up, and later start trying to sell them to some of the people in these new towns that are springing up back along the Red River. If we do that, we're gonna need more help up at our ranch. So, Alex and I would like to offer you, Cortez, and you, Ignacio, a piece of ground to build your dwellings on. We have large amounts of garden space available, a stream with plenty of fish in it that runs through the property, there's timber for wood, and lots of grasslands for stock. And, once everything is working, we could pay you a small wage for your work, you and your women folks. You interested in that?"

Cortez turned to Ignacio and spoke rapidly in Spanish. Both men nodded in the affirmative and stuck out their hands to Billy and Alex.

"Si, Senores, we would like that very much. We can work hard for you and us."

Alex grinned and shook both men's hands. So did Billy. And Alex asked one question of the two Mexicans. "Can you ride?

Again, both Cortez and Ignacio nodded. Ignacio spoke quickly and said. "Si, si, senores. We, both, know caballos, we both are vaqueros!"

"You want to find cattle, cows, vacas, senor, Ignacio and I, Cortez, can gather las vacas. Get you mucho, many vacas."

"Good. It's settled then. Go tell your women that you'll be homesteading with us."

Ignacio and Cortez nodded excitedly and hurried to tell their families.

"Billy," Alex addressed his cousin. "Cuz, like I said earlier, I think one of us should stay here with them tomorrow. Send one of the Mexican men with me back to the town for more supplies. If we travel by horseback, the two of us can make it back here by tomorrow night. Let whichever Mex goes ride one of the new draft horses and lead the other. That way we can pack all of the additional goods we need on the extra horse as well as our mounts. What do you think?"

"Sounds okay to me, Cuz. I'll get our stuff repacked in the wagon and make room for what you bring tomorrow night. I think you oughta pick up a couple more rifles and at least two more handguns along with ammo. These ol boys don't have any arms. If they're gonna be with us at the new homeplace, sooner or later, the guns will be needed."

"Alright. I'll do that. Now, lets turn in. I am sort of sleepy." Alex yawned.

"Hit the rack. I'll go tell the shorter one to go with you. Leave the big guy here with me in case I were to need him." And Billy headed to the Mexican camp.

CHAPTER TWENTY THREE

Lancers

Just before dawn, Alex and Ignacio saddled their horses, got a handful of biscuits each, mounted, and rode off toward the settlement. By noon they reined in at the general store and began securing the extra supplies along with the additional firearms and two saddles. Two hours later, they were traveling back along their trail toward the others.

A brief rain squall during the dawn hours had lessened the heat that had enveloped the prairie yesterday. Twelve days had passed since Alex and Billy had followed the surveying team toward the settlement.

"They ought to be getting back within a another week." Posey thought to herself as she leaned against the corral fence. She watched as Jessie spun out his lariat and made the toss, expertly dropping the rope's noose over the trotting mustang's head. The man ducked under the rope and moved behind the snubbing post in the middle of the corral. He braced his legs and dropped the rope around his hips, leaning into the lariat, bringing his weight to bear against the snubbing post. The tightened rope, taut against the mustang's weight sang as the horse was brought to a halt. Quick as a flash, Jessie spun his end of the lariat into two loops around the snubbing post. Easily, slowly, he approached the skittish animal and placed the palm of his hand against the horse's quivering neck, softly rubbing the animal. Meanwhile, he slowly slid a padded saddle blanket onto the mustang's back. Next, Jessie rubbed the horse's nose and quick as a flash placed the bit between the horse's teeth. He slid the bridle halter over the mustang's head and then stepped away from the horse.

The horse stood still, then casually bent a foreleg and rested his weight on the other three legs. Jessie continued to back away from the animal until his boot heel brushed up against the saddle lying on the ground. The man lifted the saddle by its horn, turned, and slowly approached the horse. The mustang's dark eye turned slightly, watching the approaching man. Again, Jessie laid his palm on the horse's neck and rubbed the animal slowly. Then in a silky-smooth motion, he eased the saddle atop the saddle blanket and moved it forward into the cradle of the horse's back. He continued to rub the horse's neck. Then, Jessie lifted the saddle fender up and looped the stirrup over the saddle horn. He pulled the saddle cinch upward and slid the billet strap through the ring and made the necessary cinch knot. Then he fastened the rear billet, checking its seating by placing two fingers between the strap and the horse's flesh. Finished, Jessie loosed the lariat loop and let it fall to the ground, pulled the reins up, grabbed the saddle horn, stepped into the stirrup, and swung onto the saddle. That's when the morning began in earnest.

Posey watched. She was always fascinated at the young man's skill with a horse. Jessie had just enough time to flash his smile at his friend's future bride when the mustang exploded.

The small stallion bowed his back and shot up off the ground all in one explosive second with all four feet off the ground. The animal striking the ground upon its descent jarred Jessie's teeth. Before he could even think, the mustang was at full gallop around the corral. Jessie sawed at the reins trying to keep the horse's head up and halt the bucking energy of the animal. Unable to unseat the rider from his back, the horse suddenly lunged to the left without turning, spun like a top, and jumped for the sky with his back bowed, screaming his horse scream. Jessie hung on. The horse landed on all four feet and began running without a pause. The rider stuck to its back. He wasn't thrown. The horse skidded to a stop and stood, legs braced, sides heaving. Jessie waited. Nothing happened. Jessie raked the horse with his spurs. The animal plunged ahead in a controlled gallop. This time when Jessie pulled in the reins, the horse came to a docile standstill. Jessie stepped down from the saddle and led the fatigued horse toward the water trough and the waiting Posey.

"That was some ride, Jessie. You make it look so easy." Posey smiled.

"Easy ride, Posey. The old boy gave up sooner than I expected. Each morning he comes around a little sooner without as much wasted time and energy. In a couple of weeks, he'll be as meek as a kitten. Probably come when one whistles even." Jessie chuckled.

"Look, Posey! Some riders just topped the rise back toward the east. That just might be Alex and your beau. Guess we'd best be getting some breakfast started. If it's them, they'll be a mite hungry I reckon. C'mon. I'll wash up and give you a hand."

Posey hummed a happy tune as she prepared biscuit dough. She spread a towel on the table, sprinkled it with sifted flour, and plopped a large lump of larded dough on the floured cloth. She used a wooden rolling pin to level the lump of dough. Grasping a five-inch-wide rounded biscuit cutter she cut a dozen perfect circles from the leveled dough and placed them in one of her dutch ovens and then scooted it to the back of the fireplace to bake. She wadded the scraps of the remaining dough pile, formed them into another lump, and repeated the process. She ended up with another 8 perfect biscuit circles. These were placed into another oven and scooted next to the iron oven placed just minutes before at the rear of the fireplace.

Herman the German entered the cabin followed by Samuel and his woman Bright Star. Bright Star immediately joined Posey in the breakfast preparations.

Herman joined Jessie on the cabin's porch and squinted at the riders atop the far-off rise. Jessie pointed at the group of riders now clustered against the skyline and said to Herman, "That look like our folks, maybe Billy and Alex, to you, Herman?"

"Nah. I don't think so. Not unless they've hooked up with some other riders, Jess."

"Sambo! Sambo, join us on the porch. Quickly." Jessie yelled.

"What it is, Jessie suh?" Sambo asked as he closed the cabin's door. "What's the ruckus for. I though y'all were on the lookout for Alex and Billy."

Jessie pointed toward the top of the mesa. "Samuel, using your good eyes does that look like Comanches or some other Indians? Who are those people?"

"They aren't Comanches...or any other Indian's. Hmmm. Jessie, I think that those might be soldiers, maybe. They're carrying lances, I think, with something fluttering from each pole, like a small flag. It isn't feathers, though, and there aren't any warbonnets. Herman, look. Those look like tall hats, maybe."

Herman spoke out. "Jessie, Sambo's right. Those aren't Indians. Watch them ride. They're coming down the mesa's slope in formation. There's a European appearance to that line, almost like mounted cavalry or lancers, maybe."

"No Europeans here, Herman. This is Texas, and its on the border with the United States. That wouldn't make much sense." Jessie said.

The men watched as the riders reached the level prairie. The line of riders broke into two advancing columns without halting and continued in formation toward the ranch buildings.

Shading his eyes, Sambo stared hard at the on-coming horsemen. Suddenly he spoke forcefully in a harsh but lower voice. "Jessie, best gather up some guns. We might need to fight. Those are Mexican lancers. And I'll betcha that their officers are European trained. The women need to be told. Do it now, there's no time to wait!"

Herman shoved the door open to the cabin and spoke loudly to Posey and Bright Star. "The approaching people are not ours. They look like Mexicans. Best stop what you are doing. Jessie's drawing water. We need to get the rifles and pistols ready, just in case. We can eat after this is over."

The two columns of lancers halted within three hundred yards of the ranch. An officer barked an order. The second rider in each column advanced abreast of the lead rider. Each successive trooper wheeled his horse in line abreast of the last advancing rider until a straight line of lancers faced the ranch yard. The officer raised his hand and shouted "Avance!"

The line of Mexican Lancers advanced at a paced walk toward the ranch house. Posey rushed to each window and closed and barred the shutters. Bright Star placed a loaded rifle beside each window. Sambo came into the cabin, retrieved Jessie's and Herman's rifles and passed them out the door to the two men along with a loaded belt pistol. They waited on the front porch, the rifle butts on the floor. The two men folded their arms and rested them atop the rifle muzzles and continued to watch the approach of the mounted military force.

Sambo and the women watched from inside the cabin, rifles in their arms, ready to be thrust through the port holes and discharged into the line of troopers if hostilities erupted.

The lancers looked sharp and capable in the bright morning sunlight. Their tall and plumed shakos were adorned with a broad polished brass plate that reflected the sun's rays. Each shako mounted a six-inch-tall red plume. The soldier's jackets were blue surmounting a red undervest. The jackets were trimmed in gold bullion. A single white crossbelt was worn from the right shoulder across the jacket and supported a wickedly curved cavalry saber suspended from each lancer's left side. An 8-foot-long lance rested in a saddle socket in front of the rider's right stirrup. It was held erect by the rider's right hand. A small red and white pennant floated beneath the sharp lance head that glinted in the sunlight. It was the pennants that the men had seen when the riders appeared on the skyline above the mesa.

The Mexican officer barked the command "¡Alto!", halt.

Some of the troopers' horses stamped their feet at the command. It was an impressive maneuver executed flawlessly in front of a lonesome, desolate cabin in an immense prairie wilderness.

The Mexican officer saluted Jessie and Herman by touching the brim of his shako. My name is Don Pedro Bermellón de la Casa de Dagón. I and my command are here in the Mexican state of Coahuila and Texas under our Constitution of 1824 with orders from President Vicente Ramón Guerrero Saldaña to verify the legitimacy of land dwellers encountered within our borders. I am here to inspect your citizenship papers, senors, along with others encountered on these holdings. May I dismount?

Jessie touched his forehead with his right forefinger in a mock salute. "By all means, Don Pedro, do step down and be refreshed. Would your men care to water their horses? If so, the well and water troughs are directly behind you over by the corral fence."

"Si, Senores." Don Pedro stepped down from his saddle and passed his horse's reins to the sergeant beside him. He turned and faced his command and gave orders to dismount and water their horses. Turning back around, he faced Herman and Jessie and said, "Do you, senores, have proof of citizenship at hand?"

Herman looked down at Jessie. Jessie nodded in the affirmative. Si, Don Pedro. We do. We were about to sit down to breakfast. Why don't you join us. We can eat and then following the meal, you can review our papers. What say you, sir?"

"Si, senores. That is most gracious. I would enjoy a meal. Do you have coffee?" Don Pedro removed his helmet and followed the two men through the cabin's door.

Jessie made the introductions. "Posey, this is Senor Don Pedro, the commander of the Mexican lancers. He would enjoy sharing breakfast with us."

Jessie turned back to the Mexican. "I'm sorry, Pedro, but we weren't expecting company this morning and I haven't anything prepared to offer your men."

"Not to worry, sir. My men have their own rations if they are hungry. It will not be necessary for your women to prepare them food. But thank you. Who are the others gathered here?" Don Pedro motioned to Bright Star and Samuel.

"These are our friends, Samuel and his wife Bright Star. We rescued them from raiding Comanches months ago. They reside with us now and help us with the ranch. Let's sit, eat, and then afterward, we'll present our papers to you." Jessie motioned toward a chair at the table.

While Poinsettia and Bright Star were serving the food, Jessie parted the curtain to the sleeping quarters and retrieved their land grant documents and the newly drawn surveyors' maps.

He placed the documents on the floor near his chair and rejoined the others for breakfast. Following the meal, Don Pedro excused himself momentarily and went to check on his men.

Jessie spoke softly to Samuel. "I'm going to show this Mexican officer our papers. While I do that, I want you to move over toward the window there, take a seat, and with a handgun out of sight, cover me just in case. We don't know much about this group of soldiers or why they're here. Do it now before he returns."

Jessie stood up and moved from the table. He drew his belt pistol and checked the priming. He holstered the gun and addressed Herman.

"Check your piece, Herman. Just keep it close by and out of sight."

"Posey, you and Bright Star clear the table and wipe it down so that I can spread our documents out. Samuel, have Bright Star flank you just in case. Remember, everyone, we're supposed to be Catholic as professing citizens of Mexico. So if you are asked, say yes. If he questions Bright Star, well, Samuel, you were stolen from Mexico, you know what to say and your Spanish is fluent, so say it right. Be convincing."

The cabin door opened. Don Pedro entered, followed by the troop's sergeant. Don Pedro looked at Jessie. "Senor, thank you for preparing the documents for me to see. That is a massive display, maps and all. This is my sergeant, Sergeant Emanuel Lopez. He can serve as our witness if we should need an inquiry. Agreed?"

Jessie and Herman nodded. "I'll speak first then." Jessie said as he pointed to the papers. "As you can see, we were granted these lands to homestead by Empressario Haden Edwards and his clerk over at Nacogdoches, that was dated right here." Jessie jabbed his finger on the paper under the date. We did that on May 19, 1825."

The Mexican officer peered at the signatures and date on the land grant. "Senor, all would appear to be in order. But if you are the Jessie Gregg as signing here, who are these other signers, and where are they presently?"

Jessie looked at Herman. "He's Herman Schiller. He signed there." Jessie jabbed his finger on the paper next to Herman's signature. "And there, that's Poinsettia, Posey Sharon Vaughn, right there. See. And below her signature are those of our partners, Alex Bowie Avery, and his cousin William Billy Rudd. They've ridden over to Nacogdoches for winter supplies.
They oughta be back any day now. Been gone for almost two weeks already. That answer your questions."

The officer rubbed his chin thoughtfully. "You seem to have all the answers, Senor, all the answers. But the other two men. You say they'll return soon?"

"Yes, Don Pedro. Some time in the next few days. Its about a nine day haul over to the settlement from here. You are aware of that, I'm sure. You are, right?" Jessie waited, breathing slowly.

"Si, si, si, senor. I am. But what about him, the black man. You haven't mentioned him. I do not see another signature on this paper. Is he a contraband? Or perhaps a runaway, a former slave?" Is he a citizen of Mexico. Why is he here now, in this cabin, with you people?"

Jessie eased his chair back from the table slightly so that he could stand if necessary. He leaned toward the Mexican officer and his sergeant. "Senor Pedro. Samuel and the Indian woman Bright Star were fleeing from some Comanches. We drove off their attackers, the Indians, and gave them shelter and a home with us. That was months ago, before we had even started construction of our ranch. They are our friends and reside here now, and work with us. Samuel is not my slave. As far as we're concerned in this cabin, on this our land, he is one of us!"

"In Mexico, Senores, in Mexico, you as a citizen must be a member of the Catholic faith. Are you, and you, and you, and you Catholic?" Pedro pointed at Posey, Herman, Jessie, and Samuel. "Are you. Speak up now. Make note of what they say, Sergeant Lopez!"

Samuel stood up, back against the wall. He looked at the Mexican commander and spoke in fluent Spanish. "Sí, mi Capitán. Si, I am Catholic, a citizen of Mexico until captured by Indians during a raid. Bright Star, she is a native, but a convert. And these people, my friends Jessie, Herman, and Posey as well as Alex and William, are professing Catholics and sworn Mexican citizens."

Jessie interrupted. "That's correct, Don Pedro. We all took the oath back in May when we acquired the land grant. It was required by your laws and Empressario Edwards. We, all that signed that document, raised our right hands and swore your oath of citizenship and affirmed our religion to be Catholic."

Don Pedro addressed Samuel in Spanish. "¿De dónde vienes? Where did you come from?"

"My home was in the state of Coahuila, in the village of Nacimiento de los Negros. Many of my people were there, given citizenship as a protective force on the northern border against the Indians. My family and others had escaped from the Seminoles of Florida." Samuel held his breath, awaiting a reply.

Don Pedro issued a command to Sergeant Lopez. "Take the black man Samuel into custody immediately. He has just admitted that he is a former slave, and as such, is likely contraband. We shall gain a reward for his return."

Lopez drew his sword and advanced on Samuel. Samuel yelled. "I'm not a slave. I'm free!" He drew his pistol and shot Lopez in the chest. The Mexican halted in midstride, grasped his chest, and looked at the blood seeping between his fingers, gasped, and fell to the floor.

Don Pedro flung the table of documents aside and dashed for the cabin's door. "To Arms, to Arms!" He yelled at his startled troopers. Jessie was right behind him with a drawn pistol. Herman shoved through the door behind Jessie. One of the lancers lunged his horse toward the cabin, lowered his lance, and pierced Jessie's stomach. Jessie screamed and stumbled, the lance protruding from his body. He leveled his pistol toward his attacker, fired, and killed the Mexican trooper.

Herman wrapped a huge arm around Don Pedro's throat and pulled him up on his toes and at the same time jammed his cocked pistol into Pedro's chest. "Order your men to stand down, damn you, do it now or I'll blow your brains all over this porch. Now, you bachelor's son! Do it now!"

At the same moment, Posey discharged a rifle through a window's gun port and blew another trooper from his saddle. Horses were milling, rearing, bucking, and the Mexicans were trying to organize and get mounted.

The Mexican officer screamed at the troopers. "Halt, halt, do not attack. My life is in danger. Stop, stop, as your commander, I order you to stop!"

His yelling was interrupted by another shot from the cabin. Samuel had discharged a musket at the mass of troopers. Another Mexican soldier fell to the ground. A lance was hurled by one of the soldiers. It struck Herman's hip, tearing away tissue and embedding itself in the cabin wall. Herman jerked Don Pedro's chin up hard. "Now, Mexican. Call them off or you're dead." And he jerked his neck hard.

"Stop, cease your attack. Gather your horses and move back from the cabin. Do it now!" Don Pedro ordered his men. At last the Mexican troopers quieted their horses, turned about, and led them from the cabin's yard. Their shakos and lances littered the ground in front of the cabin. Three Mexican troopers lay dead or dying on the ground. The soldiers withdrew several hundred yards and remounted their horses. They waited.

Herman whirled Don Pedro around to face him. The giant German was so angry that spittle flew when he spoke. You, consarn your Mexican soul, you have killed a good man, my friend. And all because of greed, an opportunity for gain at the expense of an innocent man. You deserve to die!"

Posey rushed through the doorway and knelt by Jessie. She cradled his head in her arms. The lance protruded from his body, its shaft rising almost to the porch roof. He smiled up at Poinsettia and died.

Posey's wailing cry of despair was devastating. Its sound carried to the assembled soldiers who lowered their heads. Herman tucked his pistol back into his belt and drew his belt knife. He deftly sliced Don Pedro's right ear from his head, caught it as it fell, and sheathed his knife. He grabbed the Mexican officer's hand and placed the severed ear in the open palm. "Something for you to savor on your journey home. Maybe one of your flapdoodle troopers can sew it back on for you. Anyway, don't come back this way. If you do, I'll give them your other ear while it's attached to your head. Now git!" And he shoved the Mexican off the porch and into the dirt. Samuel appeared in the doorway dragging the dead Mexican sergeant's body. One of the troopers led the officer's horse over to him, dismounted, and helped the injured Don Pedro up on his horse.

Samuel addressed the two troopers in Spanish. "You have four of your number dead in the courtyard. Bring some horses and take those dead men with you. Quickly now." The two rode back to where the remaining soldiers waited leading Don Pedro on his horse. A squad was dispatched to remove the four Mexican corpses. Then they all turned about and rode back toward the mesa and away from the ranch.

Samuel and Bright Star joined Herman and Posey on the porch. Samuel helped ease Herman into a seated position on the porch and inspected the lancer's wounding. "This must be tended to now, Herman. You bled much during the past few minutes. Posey, leave Jessie. You can do no more for him. I need a needle and thread, and a red-hot poker. Hurry now. We can save Herman. He saved us. We'll tend to Jessie's body later." Samuel spoke to Bright Star in halting Comanche and sent her for wet towels and a bucket of water. The morning was young yet.

Finis

Earned Acreage

Ted L Gragg

Ted Gragg spent an early childhood in the Blue Ridge mountains of North Carolina. Late childhood saw a move to the coast of South Carolina, a state that became a permanent home. A United States Air Force veteran, he met his wife in Texas. She, being a former resident of the high plains of New Mexico and Texas, instilled a love of the west and its adventures into their family.

Ted served the State of South Carolina as a deputy wildlife officer for the Department of Natural Resources. It was a second nature activity as he had always been a hunter, enjoying the chase through the Carolina mountains, the swampy lowlands of the Carolina coasts, and the majestic western plains and mountains.

His books relate information from these adventures. His first novel, *PUMA,* was released in 2008.

The heritage of both his and his wife's families began as American colonists from Scotland and England before the American Revolution. Following the American Revolution, both families moved westward, some ending in the Blue Ridge, some as far west as the remoteness of the Palo Duro Canyon countryside in West Texas. The opening novel of a new series, *DEFIANT CAROLINIANS,* released in June of 2023, is drawn from the beginnings of the American pageant. It is followed by the newest work and second book of the series *EARNED ACREAGE*.

Ted's life work centered around firearms and their relationship to American history. He led the search for the missing Confederate warship CSS Pee Dee by forming the CSS Pee Dee Research and Recovery Team while his wife built a museum to display the results of the team's effort. The search for the warship was successful and resulted in two massive Brooke rifled cannon and a Dahlgren 9 inch cannon being raised from South Carolina's Great Pee Dee River and placed on display at the Veterans Center known as Veterans Village of the Florence National Cemetery. This adventurous search was detailed in the books *GUNS OF THE PEEDEE, THE SEARCH FOR THE WARSHIP CSS PEE DEE'S CANNONS* released in 2011 and the later *GUNS OF THE PEE DEE, THE CANNON RECOVERY* 2018.

As a life member of the National Rifle Association, Ted served as a firearms instructor, training counselor, and a shooting range technical advisor. He and his wife Connie operated a successful firearms retail and indoor shooting range establishment for 3 decades.

Together, Ted and Connie have lived an adventure founded in trust, love, and faith in the Lord Jesus Christ. Their forthcoming third book in the *Defiant Carolinians* series *IDYLLIC DOMINION* is due for release in 2026.

Ted L. Gragg
Historian Emeritus Horry County Museum

www.ingramcontent.com/pod-product-compliance
Lightning Source LLC
Chambersburg PA
CBHW071905290426
44110CB00013B/1286